SHORT STORIES

Father

Gritty Southern Fatherhood Anthology Copyright 2024 © Gritty South

First Edition

All rights reserved under International and Pan-American Copyright Convention. No part of this publication may be reproduced or transmitted in any form or by any means, electronic or mechanical, including photocopying, recording, or by any information storage and retrieval system, without prior written permission from the Publisher.

Gritty South
GrittySouth.com

This work is based on the authors' personal perspective and imagination.

Editor and Interior Designer– Katie Warren
Publisher – Angela Broyles

Library of Congress Control Number: 2024933403

Perfect Bind book ISBN: 978-1-958273-96-8
eBook ISBN: 978-1-958273-95-1

Contents

Deer Hunting 1
Peter Last

When Your Name Is Not in the Box 15
Ann Nunnally

Hot Springs High 27
Jennifer Horne

Exhale to Ascension 28
Donna Steele

Graveyard Shift at Robsham Hall 47
Pete Black

Confronting Failure 50
Mike Wahl

A Southern Gentle Man 62
Laura Hunter

Nomenclature 92
Jennifer Horne

The List 94
Christal Ann Rice Cooper

Team Hoyt 107
Pete Black

Highway 11 110
Judy Benowitz

Dad 128
Daniel Michael

The Fishing Trip That Never Happened 138
Bill King

Super Dad 150
Pete Black

Hindsight 153
Tom McDonald

Buzzards in a Cedar Tree 170
Corinda Marsh

You've Got His Hands 187
James D. Brewer

Searching for Dad 193
Nancy Holder Pressley

Life Turning on a Dime 209

Vanessa Davis Griggs

Meet the Authors 230

Deer Hunting

Peter Last

"This hooks in here."

My dad reached around and clipped the carabiner of the safety strap to the D-ring on my harness. I knew how to do it, he'd taught me himself, but he was nervous, so I didn't protest.

"Don't take this off," he said. "Not until you're ready to get out of the tree stand."

"Yes, sir."

"If you do, you might fall and hurt yourself. Do you know how many hunters needed medical attention last year after falling out of tree stands?"

"Fifty-seven hundred," I responded automatically. Dad was right. Repetition really did make things stick.

"That means during their lifetime, the average hunter has up to a five percent chance of needing to go to the hospital from falling," Dad quoted his favorite statistic.

"Yes, sir," I replied. "I won't take off the harness unless I'm getting out of the stand."

"Good." Dad climbed down the ladder. He looked up at me from the ground and posited one more question. "What's the first rule of hunting?"

"Never shoot something you don't intend to kill," I answered. "The second one is nearly as important. Never shoot at something you can't see."

"Good." Dad fidgeted for a few seconds. "I'm not far over that way. If something happens, call for help and I'll be here in a second."

"I'll call if anything goes wrong."

It was an empty promise since I knew everything would be alright. It wasn't my first time hunting, or even my second. I had been going hunting with my dad for three years. Nothing had happened so far, and nothing would go wrong this time. He was just nervous since this was my first time in a tree stand by myself.

"Alright," he said. "I'll leave you to it, then."

He hitched his rifle a little higher on his shoulder and walked further into the woods. I heard him shuffling through the fallen leaves as he trekked down the hill the few hundred feet to his tree stand, then everything was quiet.

Dawn had broken twenty minutes prior, and nature was still shaking itself awake. I wore a second layer, a vest, to ward off the chilly November air. Still, when breezes rustled gently through the trees, they carried with them a certain discomfort.

That would change with the rising sun, the rays of which I could just start to see filtering through the bare branches of the forest. I liked the forest this time of year. Leaves no longer obscured the view in every direction, and while some might find the grays and browns of fall boring or even depressing, they soothed my soul.

Truth be told, I didn't go hunting with my dad for the sport or the meat. The quiet and solitude were my main draws. It was the only place I could sit and hear nothing, feel no stress of homework, no worries of what someone else thought of me. I was alone with my thoughts, and that was enough.

My chances of even spotting a deer were historically very low, but I set up my rifle for the off chance. I inserted the small magazine, worked the bolt to put a bullet in the chamber, and turned on the safety. From here, it was inevitable my mind would wander.

"Always focus on your surroundings," my father often said. "If you aren't paying attention, you might let the biggest buck you've ever seen get away."

This was always followed by the same anecdote of him missing a shot one time because he was dozing. Though the story is no doubt true, the antler size seems to increase with each telling.

I was okay with it, though. Killing animals and netting a fancy trophy were the farthest things from my mind.

And what fills a thirteen-year-old's thoughts when he's out in a tree stand? I tried to be spiritual, to focus on God's creation and thank Him for it, but the teenage mind is a fickle yet predictable arena. It was not long before thoughts of Heidi Jenkins popped into my head. Heidi was the prettiest, smartest girl at school, a fact some of my other friends would debate. We can't all be right, I suppose.

Heidi was a year younger than me and yet we got along just fine. My mid-pubescent brain didn't yet view her as a romantic interest, and I had no idea why she should fill my thoughts any more than Marty or Steve or any of my other friends.

A movement jolted me back to the present and I swung my rifle into position, thumbing the safety switch. The doe was no more than twenty feet away, close enough that I should have seen her earlier. I could practically feel my dad chiding me. My finger dropped to the trigger instinctively, nearly pulled it reflexively, but my father's teachings kept my muscles in check. I lifted my finger to rest once more on the trigger guard, reset the safety, and scanned the surroundings.

The woods were as quiet as ever and I didn't see anything out of the ordinary. There was no danger, no flashes of orange or tell-tale signs of other hunters, and I had a clear shot on the deer. She turned, presenting her side to me in a nearly perfect shot. I disengaged the safety once more and eased my finger onto the trigger.

The doe looked back, a signal of some sort, and two fawns bounded into view. I snapped on the safety and sat up, breathing heavily, though I don't know when that had started. I'd almost been the hunter in *Bambi*, the menacing figure with no screen time and yet one of the biggest impacts on the course of the story.

As my rapidly beating heart slowed, I watched the deer meander through my area, the fawns nibbling on food here and there while the mother watched for danger. It was a picture-perfect scene.

The wind shifted slightly, and I knew this intimate viewing of nature was at a close. The doe lifted her head, sniffing the new breeze and the scents on it. One of them was my own. She bolted, her fawns close behind, and melted into the trees in a crunching of leaves, but causing considerably less racket than you might expect.

Part of me was sad at the missed opportunity to bag a deer and bring home some meat. My father would have been proud, would have shown the picture to everyone he knew.

On the other hand, I'm glad I wasn't able to shoot. That scene, those deer walking through the forest, is a picture which has remained with me ever since. It's easily one of the most beautiful things I've ever seen.

After the deer were gone, I settled back in to wait. My mind wandered again for some time before I was jerked back to reality, this time by a crash. I scanned the trees, cocking my head and straining to hear the slightest noise. It had been a big sound, almost like a tree falling. A resonating creak surged into existence, culminating in another hideous crash, this one accompanied by a sharp cry.

"Dad?" I called. It took a few seconds for my brain to process what I had just heard. "Dad!"

I lunged for the ladder, pulled up short as I tried to descend the first rung. I struggled, pulled, jerked, trying to figure out what was wrong. In a moment of clarity, I remembered my harness and reached back to unhook the carabiner. The extra few seconds probably saved me from injury. The pause forced my brain to start working again, and I climbed down the ladder in a controlled fashion.

"Dad!" I called once my feet were firmly planted on the ground. I slung my rifle over my shoulder, grabbed a small pack from the base of the tree, and started down toward my father's tree stand. The slope was relatively steep, and the leaves and branches covering the ground made it difficult to find any purchase on the underlying soil. I slid more than walked on my way down, slamming into a few trees along the way but miraculously sustaining no real injuries of my own.

My father's silence continued despite my hails, and finding his location was harder than I expected. Only trees and hillside met my view and I searched more and more frantically. It should be right here! Then, the dark metal of the tree stand jumped out at me, ladder hanging askance from its tree. I could not see the small platform nor my father.

I had overshot my father in my frantic search and had to work my way back up, a task simultaneously harder and easier than the descent. My muscles, already burning with fatigue, struggled to push me up the slope, but gravity no longer seemed intent on pulling me off my feet and throwing me down the hill. I slipped and slid on the ground, pulling myself forward when necessary with trees and shrubs.

The tree his stand still hung from leaned sideways, the cause of this shift immediately apparent. A second tree, dead and rotting but clearly still heavy, had finally fallen, crashing into my father's tree. It lay atop the living tree, perched precariously in the branches, but not looking like it would go anywhere in the immediate future. I hoped.

Working my way around the trees, I finally spotted my father's orange hat amidst the underbrush.

"Dad!"

He didn't say anything, didn't move as I scrambled toward him. He was clearly unconscious, but that was only the first of my concerns. A huge limb from the dead tree had broken off and fallen atop him, one of its spear-like branches impaling his legs.

"Dad, can you hear me?" I shouted. I dropped to my knees beside him, slipping my rifle from my shoulder and slinging my pack to the ground near his head.

Blood already soaked the leaves around my father's leg, and panic clouded my thinking. I was halfway out of my vest before I remembered my first aid kit contained a dozen more sanitary, more absorbent items. I pulled out some gauze and ripped open the packaging, nearly sending the white material into the dirt. Bunching up the gauze, I tried to press it to the wound, but the branch prevented me. I couldn't apply pressure, and my father was bleeding out.

I screamed, tears of frustration running down my face as I watched the blood continue to leave his leg. He was going to die here because his stupid son didn't know what to do. And then I remembered.

"Massive bleeding," my father read from an index card. "What do you do?"

"Direct pressure," I answered.

"Not moderate bleeding," Dad corrected. "Massive bleeding."

Of course. I tore through my pack, throwing items to the ground until I finally emerged with a tourniquet. The blood on my hands made the packaging slick. I couldn't get a grip on the plastic to tear it open. My teeth on one side of the notch and both hands on the other side did the trick, and the small roll of stretchy material fell to the ground. I scooped it up, scrambling frantically for the end.

"Tight enough for the rectangles to change to squares," I told myself as I wrapped the tourniquet around my father's leg, a few inches above the puncture site.

The operation was simple, and in less than a minute, I had the tourniquet applied. The clothing around the wound was soaked with blood, so I couldn't immediately tell if blood was still seeping out. Though the indicators on the tourniquet said it was tight enough, I still wasted several minutes convincing myself of the fact.

What was next?

"Shock is usually fatal if left untreated." In my mind's eye, Dad sat behind a metal table and held the dreaded index cards. "What are signs of shock?"

"Massive bleeding," I muttered, rummaging through my supplies now scattered around the area. I knew how to treat shock. Just elevate the legs and cover the person. And call 911.

I grabbed my cell phone from my pocket, the thing slipping around in my bloody fingers. I wiped my hands on my pants, then cleaned the phone screen until I could see it well enough to punch in the unlock code.

No signal.

I looked around for someplace high up where I might get some bars, a tree to climb, perhaps. No, I needed to attend to my father. The chances of getting a signal out here were remote, and he would die unless I treated him correctly. Shoving the phone back into my pocket, I located an emergency blanket and unwrapped it. After shaking it several times to unfold it, I did my best to tuck it around my father's large frame.

I needed to raise his legs as well, to shunt as much blood back to the heart as possible. I did this with one of them, but the other was still pinned to the earth by a limb weighing several hundred pounds. Panic began to rise in my throat again. If I couldn't elevate both legs, was he going to die?

"Do the best you can and move on." My dad's words echoed in my mind. "Many lives have been saved by less-than-perfect treatment, but people usually die when no treatment is rendered."

Good advice. I needed to get his leg unpinned anyway. I looked at the limb on top of my father, even tried to lift it but to no avail. I'd have to cut the impaling branch off to get him out, but all I had was my pocketknife which, sharp as it was, would not be of much use against the wood.

I squatted, rapping my knuckles against my forehead, willing myself to think. There had to be something here that would work. Dad had an emergency saw in his bag, didn't he? I found his pack where he had left it, propped up against his tree stand ladder. Problem was, when the tree had been knocked sideways, it pinched and crushed the bag, pinning it in place. Even the zippers were hidden, leaving the contents inaccessible.

Not if I had a knife, I realized a moment later. The blade made short work of the tough fabric, but only a few items fell out, none of them the saw. I fished my hand through the opening, groping through the interior to extract items one by one. Many, like Dad's satellite phone, had been smashed by the tree. Fortunately, the saw was intact, and I rushed back to my father. He was still unconscious, and as I looked at his pale face, I had a horrible thought.

I never checked for a pulse or to see whether he was breathing.

Dropping down beside his head, I did both, feeling

for the artery in his neck while watching his chest. He was breathing, I noted with relief after a tense five or six seconds, and while his pulse was weak, it existed.

I sat down heavily, dropped my head into my hands, and started to cry. I had forgotten the most basic thing and it could have killed my father. I didn't know what I was doing, and he wasn't going to make it because of me.

But he wasn't dead yet, I realized. Imperfect treatment was better than none. It had saved his life so far, but right now I was doing nothing, and that would kill him. Angrily swiping tears from my cheeks, I tried to recall everything I knew. He was breathing and had a pulse. I had stopped his bleeding. Or had I? The wound on his leg was the only one I had seen, and I hadn't looked for any others.

Quickly and methodically, now more in control of my emotions, I swept his body with my fingers, feeling everywhere I could and looking for blood. Fortunately, other than the tree through his leg, he appeared to have no major injuries.

Now I could work on this branch. Unraveling the emergency saw, I fed the thin, tough wire around the branch and placed a finger through the rings on either end. I began working the wire back and forth, taking off a small line of sawdust with each pass. It would take a while, but the saw was sharp. This would work.

"Peter."

I looked around, confusion addling my fatigued mind. My father was awake, looking at me, and it took a moment for this fact to process.

"Dad!" I shouted. "Are you alright?"

"I've felt better." Dad's voice was raspy, but to hear him say anything at all made my spirits soar. "It looks like I have a stick through my leg."

"Right." I chided myself for the stupid question. "I put a tourniquet on it."

"It's a good one," Dad told me. "Looks like it's doing the job."

"I'm working on getting you out." I pointed to the branch impaling my father's leg. "I'm half-way through."

"Good work," Dad encouraged me. "What we need to do now is call for help."

"I don't have any cell service."

"I have a satellite phone in my bag."

"Smashed when the tree fell," I interrupted him.

"Well," Dad said after a moment. "It looks like you need to finish cutting through this branch. We do need to crib the limb behind me, though, otherwise it may fall once you've cut all the way through."

"Crib?" I hadn't heard the term before.

"Put stuff under it so it can't fall," my father explained. "Get the sturdiest sticks you can find, and we'll build a tower like with Lincoln Logs."

I didn't really understand, but it was good to have Dad back, telling me what to. Everything was going to be alright now. Under my father's direction, I gathered enough sticks and logs to create an overlapping support system, bracing the branch up behind Dad.

"And now, get back to cutting this branch," Dad said once I was done. "This time, though, cut down here nearer to my leg."

I obeyed, so intent on my task I did not see the pain which must have been on his face. Every stroke of the saw had to have been excruciating for him, but he never made a sound.

The tree almost pinched my saw as I finished the cut, but I jerked it free in time. My fingers were bloody from their contact with the saw's rings, but I barely felt the pain. Dad was free now.

"Not yet," he said as I reached for the branch. "You'll have to finish your first cut."

Sure enough, the weight of the limb had driven the branch down against the amputated length, once more pining my father, but this time with weight and friction. I set to work on the original cut.

I was stymied by the pain in my hands but bolstered by my father's encouragement and direction. By the time I had cut through the branch, my fingers were so stiff I had to work to uncurl them from the saw.

"Okay, get your rifle now."

I picked up the gun from where it lay nearby.

"Drop the magazine and clear the chamber."

I did this, spitting a bullet to the side. I picked it out of the dirt and leaves and put it in my pocket.

"Use the butt of the rifle to knock the segment loose," Dad said. "Then I'll be able to move."

"Won't that hurt?" I worried.

"No more than the pain I'm in now," my dad said. He placed a stick between his teeth. "Just do it and get it over with."

I smashed the butt of my rifle against the small segment

of branch I had cut out, not looking at my father. I could hear him whimper as I struck the wood repeatedly, sliding it free little by little. Finally with a last strike, the wood popped free. The limb sagged under its own weight, but the gap remained, just enough for my father to wiggle free. I helped him move his leg and extract the portion of the branch stuck into the ground. After hours of work, he was finally free.

The stick remained in his leg to help control the bleeding, and I wrapped around it with gauze and bandages.

"Take my gun and plug up the barrel," Dad instructed me next. "I'll need to use it as a crutch, and I don't want dirt getting inside."

I unloaded my father's gun, then set to work turning it into a crutch. I covered the barrel with some cardboard pilfered from a bandage box and held it in place with duct tape. Then I helped Dad to stand up, me on one side and his gun on the other.

"There's no two ways about this," he said, looking up the hill. "It's going to suck, but we have to do it. Let's get this over with."

What followed was the longest hour of my life. The trek up the hill was difficult, and I learned a lot of new words. Even once we were at the top, it was another half mile to the truck. Dad felt pain with every step, and I had to force myself to ignore it as we pushed forward, one hop at a time. The going was excruciatingly slow, and darkness had fallen by the time we arrived.

"No cell service," Dad said as he leaned against the tailgate, blue light from his phone illuminating his face in the darkness of night. "Looks like you'll be driving."

"I don't know how to drive, Dad."

"I'll teach you," Dad said as I helped him around to the passenger seat. "Just be glad this isn't a stick shift."

My dad lost his leg but he's still alive, so I guess that's a pretty good trade. They say I saved his life. I guess I did, but one thing is for sure: I couldn't have done it without him.

When Your Name Is Not in the Box

Ann Nunnally

Annie scurried up the narrow red clay path to the sidewalk adjacent to the Alberta City viaduct. She glanced back to the house she was escaping from… the house with dark secrets, fear, and pain. The weeds and vines on either side of the path were sure to have snakes and creepy-crawlers that no eight-year-old wanted to encounter. She moved quickly and prayed she would not come across any of nature's bounty. At the top of the hill, she could see freedom.

Annie was on her way to study the Bible with other girls her age at Mrs. Gallman's home. The small troupe of GAs, Girl's Auxiliary, were working on various levels of growth and the recognition program at the church was in the near future. All work had to be completed for the big event. Annie loved memorizing the scriptures and learning more about the mission outreach of the Baptist church she attended.

Although she was young, Annie was familiar with the community and loved her freedom to walk and explore. Her mom did not drive and, in fact, there was no car to even attempt learning on. Walking or catching the bus were the only options for travel, and this adventurous girl could do both.

As she walked, Annie saw the Tastee Freeze, with its delicious chocolate-dipped ice cream cones, across the boulevard. A few paces more and she would be at Alberta Baptist Church, a place of peace and safety, and if she kept walking in about fifteen minutes she would arrive at the elementary school she loved. It was a place with food, warmth, protection, and learning. The teachers were always so kind and seemed to understand that Annie lived in a difficult situation.

Today she would cross the street at the traffic light in front of the church and head up the road to her destination. As Annie waited, she smiled at Davis Grocery, the home of the one-cent bubble gum, and Alberta City Drugstore, where she picked up her mom's medicine when she wasn't feeling well. With confidence and joy, Annie crossed the street and started up the hill.

Within minutes, Annie saw the outline of an approaching figure and panic gripped her heart. It looked like her father. What should she do? Where could she hide? Would he curse her and call her horrid names as he often did? Would he be drunk or on drugs? Why was he walking down the hill? Was he on his way to hurt her mom? With each step, the anxiety grew. Annie prayed, "Lord please make me invisible or unrecognizable to this terrible man." She crossed to the other side of the road and held her breath as he approached. He looked at her with a blank stare and continued walking. Annie flashed back to the night she had sat on the sofa next to her mom while he held a gun on both of them and her mother begged for their lives. She remembered the nights they had left home running to a public place like the hospital lobby until her dad could be apprehended by the police. She remembered coming home one night, riding in the back of her older brother's truck, and seeing the front porch windows broken and the door kicked in. The blood on the porch meant he had hurt himself and not them this time. "Pause Annie," she said to herself. "You are safe. God has once again answered your prayer."

Annie could remember the day she first understood she had a father. It seemed her household was complete with her mom and three brothers. No one ever mentioned another family member and at five-years-old she didn't realize someone was missing. Annie's daily job was to go to the mailbox and bring her mother any correspondence the postman had delivered. She carefully ran across the avenue, as oncoming cars always approached quickly and there was no shoulder next to the mailbox. She would back up against the red clay wall that was covered in beautiful, old-fashioned Seven Sister roses, reach around the mailbox, and gather the contents. She would run back to the front porch where her mom waited for the daily delivery. She noticed an envelope that was different than any she had seen before. She asked her mom who it was from, and she replied, "It's from the prison. It's about your dad." Annie froze in her tracks—*I have a dad?*

As Annie fantasized about meeting her dad, she planned to dress up in her prettiest hand-me-down, put a ribbon in her hair, and dance for the daddy she had never known. She was sure he would love her, and their family was going to be perfect! Annie knew nothing of the alcohol, drugs, hatred, and depression that had molded her father into a man who could not love and appreciate a five-year-old no matter what she did to welcome him into her life. His rejection was immediate and would continue all of her life. His erratic, life-threating visits through the years would only engrave in her mind his abandonment and rejection.

One day, several years later, Annie was crying because she didn't have a father like all the other children she knew. She had started elementary school and had quickly made friends, but none of them could come over to her house as their parents were afraid of her father. She could visit them and was welcomed by many generous families, but no parent wanted to put their child in danger. Annie learned to dread the question every friend's parent asked, "What's your name and who's your daddy?" The answer sometimes meant the end of the friendship. As she sat crying about her life, the soft whisper of the Lord came, "I'll be your Daddy."

Annie had asked Jesus into her heart when she was six-years-old and had immediately begun to learn about the Kingdom of God. She didn't know a lot about church history or theology, but she knew "Jesus loves me, this I know, for the Bible tells me so. Little ones to him belong, they are weak, but he is strong." When she heard "I'll be your Daddy," she knew God was offering to take the place of a man who had forfeited his fatherhood. She knew God never made promises he didn't keep, and she knew she had just been adopted by a father who wanted her, would provide for her, protect her, and love her with an everlasting love. Annie dried her tears and became a "Daddy's girl" that day. It would be years later before she could scripturally back up her experience, but Romans 8:14-17 would plainly affirm it:

> [14] For as many as are led by the Spirit of God, these are sons of God. [15] For you did not receive the spirit of bondage again to fear, but you received the Spirit of adoption by whom we cry out, "Abba, Father." [16] The Spirit Himself bears witness with our spirit that we are children of God, [17] and if children, then heirs—heirs of God and joint heirs with Christ, if indeed we suffer with *Him*, that we may also be glorified together. (NKJV)

> [14] For all who are led by the Spirit of God are sons of God. [15] And so we should not be like cringing, fearful slaves, but we should behave like God's very own children, adopted into the bosom of his family, and calling to him, "Father, Father." [16] For his Holy Spirit speaks to us deep in our hearts and tells us that we really are God's children. [17] And since we are his children, we will share his treasures—for all God gives to his Son Jesus is now ours too. But if we are to share his glory, we must also share his suffering. (Living Bible)

Annie found herself living in two worlds: The world of havoc, grief, and pain perpetrated by sin and poverty, and the world of being a joint heir with Christ. She had to walk through her natural life of rejection and abandonment, but she also walked in supernatural provision and love as "Daddy's girl." She grew naturally and spiritually, and by the end of the seventh grade she was beginning to turn into a young lady with hopes and dreams for her own family and life. An opportunity to move to another area of the city presented itself. She could leave behind the roach- and rat-infested home of her childhood and start at a new school and find new friends. No one would know the tales of abuse, public drunkenness, and fear perpetrated by her father. It was to be a new beginning. Her mom and her oldest brother would share a small, clean two-bedroom, one-bath home. There would be a place for a garden and fresh, inexpensive vegetables. A school bus would take her back and forth to school—no more walking! Best of all, her married brother and his family would live next door. Her sister-in-law and four beautiful daughters would attend church, play, shop, and share a life of love and fun with her. Annie had never been more expectant and happy.

The call came on a Wednesday afternoon during the summer of 1965. Annie had been helping her mom cut the grass and had taken a break for a drink of water. The phone rang and Annie's father was on the line cursing, threatening, and promising a visit. He warned Annie to tell her mom not to call the police or things would be bad. Annie had never heard him so out of it. She reported the information to her mom but remarked that he would never make it because he was so ridiculously drunk he would pass out before he could get to their house. Annie was wrong. She didn't know he was being driven by alcohol and pentobarbital, also known as "yellow jackets." Several hours after the call, her father burst through the front door, ran from room to room, and then ran out the front door to the car still waiting for him.

Everyone in the house was shaken by his erratic behavior, but all were safe. Annie's grandad was the recipient of her dad's wrath that night as he beat and stabbed the eighty-three-year-old to death. Multiplied grief covered Annie's family that night as the thing most feared had happened. Domestic violence, alcohol, and drugs had taken the life of a father, grandfather, husband, uncle, and friend.

Annie cried and watched others sob for three days as the funeral plans were made. No one would ever be the same and all hope of change and restoration for Annie's father were gone. As Annie knelt beside her bed she called on the Daddy she loved. "Lord, I know you love me, and I love you. Would you please get me and take me to heaven? I know suicide is not right, but you have the power to take me to my real home. I don't like this place. I don't want to start school in three weeks and face the humiliation of being a murderer's daughter. I just don't want to live! Please, please get me!" As Annie waited nothing happened. Moments later she whispered, "Then give me the power to live this life until you are ready for me." Immediately the power of the Holy Spirit fell on Annie, a broken, desperate fourteen-year-old, and brought comfort and peace like she had never experienced. The comforter, the advocate, the helper had been introduced into Annie's life in a powerful, sovereign way. She didn't know what had happened, but she knew who had happened. The power to live was poured out like hot oil on Annie.

[25] These things I have spoken to you while being present with you. [26] But the Helper, the Holy Spirit,

whom the Father will send in My name, He will teach you all things, and bring to your remembrance all things that I said to you. [27] Peace I leave with you, My peace I give to you; not as the world gives do I give to you. Let not your heart be troubled, neither let it be afraid. (John 16:25-27 NKJV)

Annie put on her best hand-me-down and started her freshman year of high school. Every need she had for the next four years was met and she supernaturally thrived with favor and love. God had taken years of pain and turned her life into something more beautiful than she could have imagined. God's grace was perfect and abundant.

You have probably guessed by now that I am Annie. The story I have penned is true and the God I have represented is so faithful. I will forever be thankful for God's grace to me and his adoption and empowerment in my life. Thank you for sharing these moments with me.

My senior year in high school, the Lord spoke this to me: "I want you to love your father." I replied, "But Lord, I don't know how to love him, I don't know him." Then the instructions came, "Love him as you would any lost soul on the street." After a moment I replied, "I can do that, and I will." It was not easy to navigate this assignment, but again the grace was there and step by step I learned to love the unlovely as Christ does. I traded fear for love and ministered not as a daughter but as an ambassador for Christ.

After the death of my grandfather, my father was placed in a mental hospital for the criminally insane. I visited him, gave him a Bible, and took my mom to see him. When I was engaged, I took my future husband to meet him and tell him of my plans for marriage. He had been removed from the mental hospital and placed on trial for murder. He was at the county jail awaiting his transport to prison, and I took my children to meet him. When he was released from prison, we visited with him again before he left for Wyoming. Out West, his behavior was repeated, and he was placed in a mental hospital for shooting and wounding a man during an altercation. Several heart attacks and poor health landed him in a nursing home. Through the years I established communication with his caregivers and sent money for clothes, snacks, and personal needs. He never knew the support was from me.

In 1998, I was given an all-expense paid business trip to Colorado Springs, CO. I prayed about going and realized I would be a short flight across the Rockies to the nursing home where my earthly father was spending his last days. It had been eighteen years since my last face-to-face. All my life I had prayed that God would send someone to share the plan of salvation with him and make sure he was ready to step into eternity. Little did I know it would be me!

I arrived at the nursing home, and the doctors and nurses I had conversed with for years greeted me warmly. They directed me to the dining hall where my dad and his friends were eating. I looked at my dad, called him by name, and said hello. He said nothing. His friends commenced asking about me. He said nothing. The full force of his rejection took my breath away and I almost fainted. Somehow, I spoke jokingly, "He didn't tell you about his good-looking daughter?" As they mumbled amongst themselves, I stepped to the window and cried out to my heavenly Daddy for courage to complete my mission. As I walked back, I was reminded that his salvation, not my feelings, was the thing most important.

We walked back to his room, and he settled in his bed. He did not look like the formidable terror from my childhood but like a tired old man who could barely walk and breathe. He began to ask me questions about family members, and I answered openly and honestly. When he got to the end of his questions, I told him I had two questions I wanted him to answer. First, "When you die, where do you want to be buried and do you have any specific requests?" Secondly, "When you die, do you know where you will spend eternity?" He told me his burial wishes and I told him I would do my best. Then he told me he knew he was forgiven. He had prayed the prayer of salvation with a television preacher, and he had received God's forgiveness for all the things he had done in his life. I was overwhelmed and so thankful for God's faithfulness to me!

One of the ten commandments in the Old Testament says, "Honor your father and your mother, that your days may be long upon the land which the Lord your God is giving you" (Exodus 20:12 NKJV). It is the only commandment with a promise—long life to those who honor their parents! It is quoted two times in the Old Testament and eight times in the New Testament. It is an integral part of the life of a Christian. According to Meg Bucher of biblestudytools.com, "The contextual definition of Old Testament honor (the Hebrew word *kabod*) means heavy or weighty. To honor someone, then, is to give weight or grant a person of position respect and even authority in one's life. In the context of Exodus 20:12, it means to prize highly, care for, show respect for, and obey."

God gave me the grace to add weight, position, and value to my father's life even though he didn't want it from me, nor did he deserve it. God asked me to be like him, a "Daddy's girl" representing redeeming love and forgiveness.

In November of 2000, the telephone rang, and the nursing home staff informed me that my earthly father had died. They planned to send him back to Tuscaloosa for his interment. I asked them to give the clothes I had bought to someone who needed them. They were to send me his most personal effects. About a week later, the box arrived and I placed it in the corner of my office unopened. I said I was waiting for another member of the family to open it with me. But in truth I was afraid of what I would find, or not find, among the personal effects of this eighty-nine-year-old man. It took several years to set up a date with my remaining brother to open the box. Together we looked at his cowboy boots, his razor, his Bible, and a few other items. What we both had hoped for was to find our names, a photo of us, or any mention from the man who fathered us that we had been important to him. It was not there. It was the final rejection. My name was not in the box.

The pain was short-lived, as I knew my name was where it belonged. It was written in the Lamb's Book of Life. My Father God and my big brother, Jesus, had made sure of its eternal location. Through all the years they had been faithful promise-keepers and protectors. They had never abandoned me or rejected me. I had been adopted into the eternal family of God by the shed blood of Jesus Christ. The Holy Spirit had been my comforter, helper, teacher, and friend all my life. It didn't really matter that my name was not in the box. It was written in heaven!

Today, I serve the Lord as an ordained minister and travel nationally and internationally proclaiming the truth of God's word. I have been married to my husband for fifty-three years. I am the mother of two sons and two daughters-in-grace and am a grandmother to seven grandchildren. What was meant for evil in my life was overcome by the love and mercy of God, who named me "Daddy's girl."

Hot Springs High

Jennifer Horne

You wore the ring on your right hand,
the boy from Caddo Gap made good.
You drove us through the old neighborhood.
You'd saved to buy that modest band.

The high school boy was now a man,
ready to live as a man should.
You wore the ring on your right hand.
The boy from Caddo Gap made good.

Now it is mine. Now I can,
in its light heft, feel how it stood
for all you'd done, and all you would.

Turning it idly to ponder, plan,
you wore the ring on your right hand.
The boy from Caddo Gap made good.

Exhale to Ascension

Donna Steele

The discarded ashes of his cigarette moved in the ashtray, a slight movement forward and back as the breeze from the distant fan shifted the current of the room. He watched the ashes idly, thinking about nothing, emptying his mind before he headed home. The drive took him thirty minutes past office buildings, industry, the suburbs and finally to the tiny home he occupied with his wife, five daughters, and son.

The home bespoke the failure of the man. It needed painting. There were reminders of unfinished projects both inside and out. His Dodge barely fit in the small garage. The kids' rooms were tiny, homework was done at the dining table—he had no office of his own. The absence of space dictated his life at home, most of it spent in front of the news or the paper.

The mutt he and Janie acquired at the pound was perfect for this setting. It, too, was not properly tended, a needy, bristly body walking awkwardly towards him for a pat, its hindquarters shifting left then right, tail wagging, eyes locked on his in expectation. He doubted his faint pat would satisfy the dog and he doubted, too, the dog's place in their lives. The girls never played with her, and his son wasn't a fan of the outdoors, unlike him.

The Father bent down, petted the dog, loosened his tie, and opened the door. On the other side was Janie in her red lipstick and heels, most of the girls lined up beside her, all smiling, welcoming the Father home. He said his hellos, mustering excitement in his voice to see them. Before a minute had passed, he was at his closet and dressed for running.

The weather changed from hour to hour at this time of year, and he wasn't expecting the coolness of the early evening. He put on his jacket, said goodbye to the kids, and headed for the lake. A flat path surrounded the lake, static as the day. Three times around and he would achieve his goal of three miles then head home for supper.

The routine was the same every night. The only difference was which child would need help with homework on his return, usually math as none of them excelled in this subject. He hoped his son would have followed in his footsteps, but he couldn't memorize the multiplication tables. How could he follow him in engineering?

Janie cleaned the dishes while the Father read the evening papers. When he was done, he retired to the den to watch the evening news. Most often, one of the girls would talk through it and he would correct her rudeness, sometimes harshly. He liked quiet. He liked being left alone. When the news was over, it was time for the Twilight Zone which he allowed the older children to watch. As Janie got the younger ones ready for bed, he finished the paper, checked the coffee table for his pen, his magazines, his list.

He checked his list. These things he wanted to do: walk the Appalachian Trail; watch a rocket launch from Cape Canaveral; run the fastest mile; see the sun set in the Rockies. None had been crossed off. His days were too full for daydreaming, and he had only this list to remind him of the young man he had been.

There was not enough time in the day to do any project at work to completion. Deadlines loomed; his subordinates were inadequate to the task; communication failed him.

To compensate, the Father worked overtime. His Saturdays were often spent at the office, while Janie shopped with the children and kept the house. Sundays were for church, chuck roast, and making love. He looked forward all week to Sunday afternoons he shared with Janie, shades closed, the children occupied with Sunday funnies and stuffed from lunch, too tired to bother them, the time with Janie all his.

Then Monday, and it began all over again.

When he was young, the Father dreamed of being a mountain-climber, the hill in his backyard Mt. Kilimanjaro. His brother and sister assisted him in scaling the rugged cliffs looking out for white tigers, making fires and preparing hobo meals in tin foil. Their trio swam rapids, made camp, climbed high, but only he made the summit. He placed his flag made from dungarees and felt king of the world at the hill's top. He could see into the future in those moments, and it was heady.

Before the children were born, his list made sense. The Father was a real man then, doing manly things. He took physical risks, braving sub-freezing temperatures to see a nighttime snowfall in the mountains. Driving himself to the hospital when he'd sliced his fingertips off making a piece of furniture.

He was the life of parties: dancing, flirting. He once wore a lampshade on his head.

He had been the apple of Janie's eye. She watched him drive, watched him study, watched him lift weights, watched him run. But it all changed with the first one. She came suddenly and thereafter he was no more. The young man became the Father; the partygoer became the provider; the adventurer became the company man. In a duality of gratitude and resentment, joy and fear, groundedness and wanting to take flight, he accepted her into his arms, afraid as he had never been before.

The rest of the children followed as night follows day. With each, the Father thanked his good fortune while knowing he had dug himself deeper, committed now to a family of four, then five, six, seven, eight. He remembered the joke: Why is ten afraid of seven? Because seven eight nine. Fatherhood was eating him alive, Sundays with Janie the only real pleasure of his week. Family planning as elusive as world peace, the children kept coming.

One evening, a school night, his rebellious child lied about finishing her dinner. The evidence was in sight: the contents of her plate sitting on top of the garbage. He became enraged and gave her a whipping she would remember. His children were not raised to be liars. If there was anything the Father hated, it was lies.

The Father also couldn't abide stupidity. He would go over and over the same thing with their homework, but he couldn't make them understand. He suspected they weren't listening to him. Or didn't care, and this, too, enraged him.

He remembered getting out of control when one of them couldn't write the number three: time and again, the toddler would write it backwards, no matter how patient he was. He wasn't proud of it, but he snapped the last time he watched the pen begin at the top of the number and curl the line left instead of right. Janie came running from the laundry when she heard the call-and-response of his yelling and the toddler's cries. But it didn't stop at yelling; he was rough with the child.

He spent more time at the office after that, coming home later than normal. His absence did not seem to bother anyone, even Janie. Even though he was the provider, the head of the household, it didn't amount to much in the end. His burden was his to bear and bear alone.

The Daughter

The contents of the office she knew so well she felt she was at home. The thriving plants at the window had absorbed the light for many years in that sunny and best location. The silver orb reflecting everything near it, not requiring ornament or design. The brilliant and clean cut-glass vase held the flowers, which added color to the room every week.

She was most drawn to the mahogany mantel clock. It sat atop the modern credenza but was old-fashioned, analog. The face glass was convex and irreplaceable; the hands were meticulously snipped from sheet metal with a nod to Art

Nouveau. The clock made the faintest sound as it made its way around the face. The tick, tick, tick reminded her of something she couldn't put her finger on. But it was soon forgotten as her session began in earnest with Dr. Binder.

The Daughter thought of Dr. Binder as her friend though she knew this was discouraged. Together they explored her naked self one therapy session at a time. She was able, there, with her, in the sunshine of an afternoon, to remember things she had folded and placed in a compartment of her mind never to be opened. The problem was these memories were exploding the compartment drawer making it hard to shut. Some were spilling out into her everyday life and demanded to be relived, teased out like Pinocchio on the worktable.

These memories felt like a tingling of the spine as when a stranger stands too close. She viewed them as tidbits of a past she needed to come to terms with. They expressed as a shudder, a nervous tick, a scowl when none was called for. They were a ticking time bomb hidden beneath the surface. She heard the direction of the sound but could not find the damn thing.

The memories remained shrouded in mist to her rational mind. They weren't quite decipherable even though she had trained herself to remember her dreams on waking and wrote them in the most sacred of places: her journal.

The Daughter's one hour per week with Dr. Binder was the highlight of her week. She knew this was a sad statement on her life. Viewed differently, maybe she had replaced the Church with these sessions. She certainly got more out of them.

As a young girl, she questioned the gender hierarchy of man as first-class citizen and head of the household. She herself would not be a second-class citizen and didn't like being ruled. Although this concept of women being inferior was beaten into her, it would not stick—no matter how hard her father tried.

***

Dinner was not going well. James was not a great conversationalist. The Daughter was skimming the surface for things to talk about but realized she needed to go deeper to engage him. Putting her wine glass down, she propped both arms on the table and asked:

"Did you know I'm doing dream analysis?"

"That's crazy interesting! I know a little about that!"

"Want to hear one?"

"Oh, yeah! I love this stuff!"

The Daughter expounded: "I was a little girl walking in a field on the edge of a forest, maybe I was four. I was afraid to go into the forest and stayed in the field because of a butterfly that caught my attention. I also liked the sunshine. The colors of the field were bright, and the flowers were unusually tall. But the butterfly flew into the forest, and I followed it without thinking. Immediately, the butterfly turned into a stinging wasp and dive-bombed me. I shrieked and ran in circles to get away from it. I remember going deeper into the forest. I ended up being lost and couldn't get out of the brambles and saw a creature I'd never seen before, a scary one, and then I woke up. Terrified."

"Okay," said James, "who is the person you most feared when you were little?"

"Is 'Everyone' an apt answer?"

"No, narrow it down."

"Growing up, my siblings and I were afraid of our father. We were nervous when he came home from work. I was pretty much afraid whenever he was around."

"That's it," James said with Dr. Google authority.

"Spare me your analysis," the Daughter replied, leaning back to make room for the waiter's reach. "That's low-hanging fruit and I'm not sure if "Everyone" wasn't the better answer. My sisters teased me to tears and I couldn't express it to anyone, except Mom, and she was usually half out of it with Bloody Marys by noon.

"Ouch," empathized James.

"Yes, ouch."

***

Reflecting on the evening as the Daughter unwound with a glass of wine, snuggled into her bed—alone—she thought James wasn't worth the effort she'd put into him. He was bossy. He ordered for her. And he insisted on her having dessert when she told him she wasn't hungry. He practically force-fed her. On to the next one.

At her late age, not quite forty but looking like twenty-five, she could get dates, but they did not turn into lasting relationships. It was easy to find fault with men. They generally talked about themselves only and needed propping up and fluffing out.

The last one was fun to be with, but his hands were too soft.

The one before that loved sports too much.

She saw one get angry and that she couldn't abide. He was out.

Roan was the man that least resembled her Father, and she'd been closest to him. He was an easy-going sort, knew his way around the world and every hip place in town. He was in finance and had lots of money to throw at their good times dining, dancing, traveling. But Roan was not the marrying kind, which is why she'd chosen him.

To the last man, surprisingly, none of them scared her. Some of them even made her feel safe. This was an unusual feeling, as she'd felt afraid most of her life. In her dreams it wasn't just the butterfly who meta-morphed; the men in front of her—their heads--would suddenly turn into growling, barking Doberman Pinchers. Black with teeth bared, they were angry with her. She'd had this dream her entire life, and it never became less terrifying.

She listened to her alarm clock ticking. In her bedroom at this late hour, the ticking comforted her. She'd had the clock since childhood, and it was one of the only artifacts she'd dragged with her to college and beyond. That, and her Raggedy Ann.

Now that she had a house of her own, these relics from a childhood which resembled bruised fruit more than The Brady Bunch were sometimes hard to look at, but she couldn't part with them. The Raggedy Ann she'd received—aged five—as a gift from her Mother for enduring a tonsillectomy. The clock was gifted to her from her father. It wasn't one of the better ones he collected, but she appreciated this rare gesture of being singled out by him. And not in a bad way.

Most often when he noticed her it was because she hadn't pleased him. She was too loud or didn't keep curfew. He wanted their home to run like the precision of a clock but of course it never did. What two-bath house with eight people living in it could? Noise was made, tempers flared, punishments inflicted.

On her parents' deaths she knew she'd have many collections to sort: piles of sock dolls the Mother made; glass vases adorned with gold brushstrokes; minted coins; the clocks the Father stockpiled. In their tiny home he insisted on making room for a Grandfather clock. That would be the first thing to go.

Dr. Binder wanted to explore her inability to have long-term relationships. The Daughter wanted one desperately as her biological clock ticked louder and louder. Formerly, she had measured her life by boyfriends: John was the Age of Wonder; Harden was the Age of Debauchery; Pierre was the Age of the Exotic. But as the relationships became shorter and shorter, Ages were reduced to the nights of Tom, Dick, or Harry. Another sad statement about her life.

Time was running out for her to be a mother. Often, she found herself absent mindedly staring at fathers and their young children. She wondered what it felt like to be so complete, so loved.

The good ones were already married at her age. The ones she was left to filter and sort never measured up. Where does love come from, she asked herself? Where does it go? She soon fell asleep, her wine glass dropping to the floor.

> *She was pursued by a faceless man holding a timepiece in his hand. She ran from him. She slipped onto a moving train which morphed into an airplane. Still, she was pursued. She jumped. The man was with her*

in the air. Watching. The multi-colored stars pierced the darkness of the sky. One by one they dimmed then disappeared. The sky became blacker. She continued falling in a panic, saved eventually by a low-hanging cloud with a Raggedy Ann grin.

When she startled awake, she was sweating. This was worth sharing with Dr. Binder. Who was this man? Why did he scare her so?

The Son

Favoring his right side, the Son twisted into a grotesque shape to avoid being touched by the out-going passengers. He disliked the potentially infectious throng breathing all over each other, bumping fronts to backs, arms to arms. His countenance was stoic, only slightly grimacing, and resembled a comic-book villain.

Finally, the last wheezing and coughing passenger de-boarded and it was safe for him to exit the plane into the near-empty terminal. He was one of the few pilots who liked flying the red-eye shift because he liked the airports devoid of people. He saw very few of them as he briskly walked from the terminal to the parking lot where she was waiting.

The beauty he'd just purchased was a collector's dream. Seamlessly engineered side panels, front and back bedecked with chrome which reminded him of his mother's kitchen as a child, chrome holding the laminate in place with well-placed tacks spaced regularly along the edging. The car's chrome amplified the sleek lines of the Corvette's design.

The Son marveled the horsepower of the car, the heft, it's elegant fenders and taillights begging for a touch like a cat lifting its backside to the hand. Caress me, it said.

The sky didn't dim until he was well off airport property, speeding down the super-highway which earlier had carried thousands to their dinners, trucked goods to gaping bays, hustled bad boys to places they shouldn't go. The highway, with its precision lines and engineered concrete, conveyed husbands to wives and mistresses alike, served the cop and the speeder. The road had no restrictions for anyone who followed its center line nor judged the destinations to which they were heading. The road was indiscriminate, unfeeling, and devoid of judgement. It required speed only. To get from one place to the next.

The sky lacked visual cues of order. Its vastness could not be comprehended, its moods were as changing as the clouds that inhabited it: heady and charging, then shapeshifting to the thinnest chiffon veneer. It was mastered by an instrument panel of coordinates, radar, and bleeps, abstractions of planes moving at speeds of hundreds of miles per hour, reduced to blue or white dots on a black screen. This, too, the Son valued as he did the car's trajectory down the center line towards unknown places.

Speed was, for the Son, a means to an end. He didn't speed for speed's sake, but to account for leaving the abyss of the sky and its dimensionless form where he felt untethered. Revving the engine to top performance, smashing the pedal to the floorboard with no thought of letting up, titillated the Son to distraction. He was creating the void, leaving others in his rearview window, wedding speed to isolation.

He thrived in this rarified state, as alive in these moments as when he turned the airplane's nose up, climbed the sky, breaking free from the laws of gravity and other earthbound concerns.

The Son could tune out all but the essential communications aimed at him. Piloting afforded him the status he craved, the authority he liked wielding, and the freedom from others he required. The women could fill the coffee cups and make the drinks on board, attend to blankets and earbud distribution. His was a mission every time that far exceeded the banalities of what took place in the cabin. Early in his career he feigned interest in the passengers, delivering his pasted smile to the least of them. Then, he realized this was not a job requirement for someone of his stature, and he ceased the habit. The stewardesses liked it better that way and did not report his aloofness up the chain of command.

The Son preferred life to run like a well-oiled machine: there were no close calls with his landings. He wanted no predicaments, complexities, or emergencies. He buttoned-up his routine to an exacting schedule, quick pace, flawless execution.

The car glided off the interstate and onto the unlit State Road. Decelerating on the off-ramp then hitting the gas again, The Son sped his car on the darkening road, enjoying the night air as his window hummed down at the touch of his finger. The air was thick with the scent of honeysuckle. Over the hum of the engine, he could hear the deafening bleeps of insects. He watched the black trees turn to silvery green as his car lights passed them.

Slamming the brakes is what saved him and the two-hundred-pound buck standing in the middle of the road. The car did a 360, skating on the asphalt at seventy miles per hour, catching the shoulder, jerking into the rough, out of control until the Son pumped the brakes enough to edge the car to a stop fifty feet from the deer.

Breathing heavy, the Son opened his car door, eyes on the majestic buck. It didn't run, simply stood watching the Son with an aloof air. Exiting the car, the Son knelt, panting, held in thrall of this creature whose muscular body and crowned head was in stark contrast to the road's linear and disappearing trajectory behind it. The buck eyed the Son.

The brain cells of the Son's mind arranged themselves into the memory of that early fall morning on the stand in the woods when he was a child. Mississippi, somewhere far off the road, deep into the fields and then forests of the wild land. The place where men were men and boys became men, killing for sport and food, passing the torch to eager young sons as had been done for millennia. The instinct of domination was passed down, too.

The Father's friend had invited him and the Son to travel across the state line to spend time in his hunting camp. This chill and frosty morning they had risen early to be in the stand before the sun was up.

After an eternity of waiting, the sun broke. The deer lick had done what it was supposed to: they could hear the approach of a large animal breaking branches while foraging. Their breath abated. The young Son sensed the change: pulses quickened, the air electrified, the relaxed manner of the men jerked to high alert. He knew to do the same and did.

Until the spider began ambling up his leg.

It was not a daddy-long-leg that he'd often dangled in the bathtub to tear its legs off one at a time. It was not a small spider to snuff out with the palm of his hand. It was the juicy, meaty spider of nightmares with fuzzy legs crawling up his pant leg. The son did an inventory of all the things that could go wrong if this spider made it to his bare flesh, as his hands weren't covered as he'd forgotten to pack his gloves.

He could get an infection that would never heal. His fingers could turn black and fall off. He could turn into a spider himself and wake up one morning to find his limbs furry and black. No one would like him.

The spider inched closer. So did the buck, but the Son had lost all interest in the buck as he was in a death-match with a monster only inches from inflicting a mortal bite. How would he kill it? He would have to be quick.

Standing abruptly while simultaneously stomping his leg and screaming at the top of his lungs, the spider fell off. The buck ran too fast for a shot to be properly aimed, gone in an instant. Now all eyes were on him.

"Dumbass," his father spit out as he assessed the situation. "Can't you do anything right?"

In the present, staring at him was a buck all out of proportion. Oversized, unafraid, humiliating him as the Father had. None of his accomplishments mattered now. He was eight years old again, withering under the gaze of the Father. He'd tried to outrun his feeling of worthlessness, but here it was, epitomized by a twenty-point beast.

Ascension

The Father laid in repose, comfortable in the rectangular room in the boxy building that housed the dying. The magnolias, azaleas, and other staples of the Southern landscape belied the starkness of the interiors. Besides a nod to classical art with gold-framed prints, some well-placed homilies about heaven and peace, his was a barren room save for his family that kept vigil while he slowly let go.

His fingers had the bluish hue unique to the dying. His children didn't know if he could hear them, but they cooed kind words and happy memories into his ears anyway. Some of his offspring cherished the time they still had with him; others understood the need to be with him at his final rite of passage, but on scanning their memory banks could not recall the happy times.

This night, his last, the Son and the Daughter kept vigil.

"Glad you could make it," she said with honey-tinged-with-bitter in her voice.

"Don't give me a hard time," he replied. "I've been behind all day. Anyway, sorry for being so late."

"It's okay. I've had my quiet time with him and said my goodbyes. It's nice to see his face relaxed, sort of smoothed out. He seems approachable now which is sadly ironic."

"He does look pretty docile," the Son noted. He sat down near the bed. He gazed at the Father for a long minute. Finally, he reached out to him touching his arm. "I can't believe this is happening. I don't think I'm ready."

"It's time," the Daughter sagely replied. She had been witness to the Father grimacing in pain, slowed by age, lost sometimes in place and mind. She had forgiven him long before The Son even considered it, if he ever really had. Her brother had been an enigma to her since adulthood and she rarely saw him. She had no idea who he had become besides an airplane pilot. She observed the trappings he'd accumulated, everything state of the art right down to the bow and arrow he used to hunt deer. She studied him, finally asking, "Do you remember our trips to the beach?"

The Son replied, "Barely."

"Do you remember when you brought your first girlfriend home and Dad fell all over himself trying to impress her? I thought I'd die laughing! He never could resist the beauties!"

"Yeah, 'Can I get you another scoop of ice cream? I churned it just for you!'"

"Mom knew the deal. She just rolled her eyes. She'd seen that act a time or two!"

***

Sarah was the girl he'd dreamed of for his son. (His lips flinched in a paroxysm of joy). *The day August brought her home was Africa hot. Though the patio he had designed was shaded by dogwoods and the walnut tree, he couldn't escape the sweat and mosquitos. His arm ached as he churned and churned the eggs, cream and sugar, waiting for it to morph into the delight of his offspring.*

The Father recalled the happy times his family spent around the picnic table. August always tended by one of the girls. Janie serving up corn on the cob and coleslaw while he manned the grill.

He had missed Janie for years but saw glimpses of her now.

She was waiting for him. She was so beautiful in these moments, silent but beckoning. He remembered her awkward ways as a new wife and her metamorphosis into a capable mother. She had such a way with the children. Soft, yes, but he made up for that. He had been the disciplinarian. Hardly had to, though, as he remembered being a loving father.

He'd brought home the bacon and Janie did everything else. She made life so easy for him. Embracing her now was all he could think of.

August had come home at last. His awkward, clumsy boy had turned into a real fine man. He hoped his son knew how proud he was of him. And here was Andrea at his bedside. She was a caregiver beyond compare and a fine companion, too. Of all the girls, she gave him the hardest time, but he barely remembered that now. He reflected on her success in business, and it made him proud. He wished she would find a husband, but soon it would no longer be his concern.

He remembered when she was born. Janie had an easy time of it with the others, mostly, but Andrea was reluctant to poke her head out. The doctor came to him several times in the wee hours of the morning to give updates on Janie and the baby. He came to resent the baby. He wanted Janie to live above all else.

He gave Andrea a clock when she was ten, something he hadn't done for the other children. He hoped she'd understood she was being treated special. As he lay dying, he realized he had resented her for being so stubborn to appear, for causing Janie such pain, for causing him to believe he would lose his beloved. Maybe that's why they didn't get along when she was younger.

But Janie beckoned him now. With a rumbling exhale, he went to his North Star.

***

After a long pause, August, wondered aloud if his father's life was well lived. He died and lived without much ado: his friends all died before him. the only thing left standing of his legacy was an angry son and daughter, the rest of them too blind to know what their father had cost them.

Andrea considered this remark. It was clear August hadn't forgiven the Father. She hesitated, then revealed her secret to him. She was carrying twins. Being a single mother something she could do. She had escaped her past to make room for her future. She would name the babies for her father and mother, constant reminders to her of loving through the pain.

Graveyard Shift at Robsham Hall

Pete Black

"If a man is called to be a street sweeper, he should sweep streets even as Michelangelo painted or Beethoven composed music or Shakespeare wrote poetry. He should sweep streets so well that all the hosts of heaven and earth will pause to say, 'Here lived a great street sweeper who did his job well.'"
—Martin Luther King Jr.

3:00 a.m., April 9, 2016 - Robsham Theater Arts Center, Boston College: The campus is quiet and deserted. Fred, the graveyard shift janitor, pushes his yellow cart carrying his mop, broom, and cleaning supplies from room to room. His job is monotonous and not real challenging, but it provides Fred with the means for a better life for his five children.

Although the job would be demeaning to many people, for the past fifteen years Fred has been happy to have steady work with good benefits. His janitor job is less physically demanding than his previous job as a cafeteria cook at Boston College (BC).

Fred Vautour grew up in Waltham, Massachusetts, about twelve miles from Boston. There was no money for him to attend college and he wasn't interested in school anyway. At age fourteen, Fred started washing dishes part-time at Ritcey's Seafood Kitchen in Waltham. Two years later, he was promoted to a full time cook position and later became the restaurant manager. Fred worked at the restaurant for twenty-seven years.

In 1994, Fred landed a job cooking at Corcoran Commons—a huge student cafeteria at Boston College. It was the first job he ever had with paid benefits like vacation and healthcare coverage. Fred discovered a few months after beginning work that children of employees could attend the university tuition-free, as long as they met the rigorous entrance qualifications. With a required minimum ACT score of 30 or a 1300 SAT score, only 30% of those who apply are admitted to the prestigious Jesuit Catholic Research University.

In 1998, Fred was coaching his son's baseball team when his oldest daughter, Amy, showed up at the field with a handful of maroon and gold balloons. Fred knew immediately—Amy had been accepted as a student at Boston College. He proudly framed the acceptance letter and hung it on the wall at their house.

With scholarship money, Amy's annual cost to attend Boston College was reduced from $65,000 a year to $3,000 a year. She graduated in 2002. Fred encouraged his other four children to set their sights on Boston College. Oldest son John was next to be accepted and graduate, followed by Michael and then Thomas.

Cooking for 2,300 students was tough, demanding work, particularly as Fred got older. So in 2001, he took a job as the night shift janitor at the Robsham Theater Arts Center, a complex that included a 570-seat theater, classrooms, and a dance studio. Each night Fred meticulously cleaned the facility.

In May 2016, Fred's youngest child, Alicia, earned her nursing degree from Boston College, becoming the fifth child to earn a degree there. Before Alicia was presented with her diploma, sixty-two-year-old Fred Vautour was called to the stage and given the honor of presenting Alicia with her diploma. It was an emotional day for Fred and his wife Debra, who had a child at BC for eighteen consecutive years.

Over the years, the Vautours created a Boston College hall of fame room in their house with each child's college acceptance letter and diploma proudly displayed. All five kids lived on campus and often stopped by and visited with Dad as he cleaned Robsham Hall. Michael, now a mortgage writer at Wells Fargo, remembers bringing some friends by one night to meet his dad. He told them, "Meet my dad who works graveyard shift and sacrifices so I can afford to go here." One friend was so moved that he hugged Fred's neck.

Today, seventy-one-year-old Fred Vautour is retired from his days of scrubbing floors, emptying trash, and polishing the mirrors at Robsham Hall. He's proud of the five college degrees his graveyard shift job helped provide. "I loved my job," Fred says. "Being on a college campus kept me young."

Confronting Failure

Mike Wahl

The entrance to the tunnel was just a few hundred feet ahead of the Harley, which had been pulled over to the shoulder. Its powerful purring was the only sound in the clear dawn air. To the right, the sun silhouetted the mountains on the distant horizon. From this height, there was an unimpeded view, and the people who lived in the valley basin below would see no sunshine for another two hours.

Those people were well adjusted to late sunrises and early sunsets, with the extra hours of daylight without direct sun added on each end. Mark Curtis lived there, but now he straddled the Harley at the roadside, facing the tunnel. He had stopped here to let his ears have a chance to let air pressure equalize after the steep mountain climb. There was no traffic either entering or exiting the cave-like opening at this time of day, and it was great to have this world of nature all for himself. The electric line climbing the hillside to provide power for the lights inside was the only other indication that humanity held any claim on this remote mountain route.

Mark Curtis had helped install that power line during the first few years of his fifty-year tenure with Addison Electric.

From the substation near the dam in the valley below, the wire climbed the mountainside. It was too steep and rugged for any motorized equipment to navigate, so helicopters and manpower had furnished all the effort.

It had been the first job Mark had worked, just out of high school. When he had applied, he was hired immediately for the duration of the contract. Few others were willing to dedicate years of their lives struggling to overcome such obstacles on a desolate mountainside. To be closer to the work, he had moved to Vantage, one of seven villages located in the valley. But, once that project was completed, Addison had offered him a permanent job, so that had been the only employer he had ever known.

A few years after moving to Vantage, Mark had met and married a local girl named Allison Curly. The similarity of her name to that of his employer had seemed to Mark to be an omen. Of course, that wasn't the only reason Mark had married Allison. Her long blonde hair had been an enticement since the moment he first had seen her in Maggie's Diner. On the other hand, he was basically married to Addison Electric, because he was so deeply indebted to the company for the opportunity he had been granted, and the job he loved so much. Although he had been so often away from home, he loved his family, but he had to admit, he had not been a great father for their four kids.

It wasn't that he ever ran around on Allison, he was thinking as he faced the looming mouth of the tunnel. But just like the tunnel, he really didn't know what all was hidden inside of her. He had spent so much time working over the years that he felt instinctively that he had missed out on too much with his family along the way.

It had become a burden for him recently, finally nagging him so much that he had to admit that he had been a lousy husband and father to his real family. Addison had been a great employer, but when push came to shove, that relationship didn't really possess the qualities of family life that a wife and children could provide. This guilt was what had led him to this very spot at this very time. Yet, in reality, this motorcycle venture was just a furthering of his faults. He knew now he was running instead of trying to amend his broken past at home. How in the world could he be so selfish? How could he realize his selfishness, and not stay to try to make things better at home?

In the back of his mind, over the years, Mark had developed a certain perspective about tunnels. It was a combination of fear for all that could go wrong, along with admiration for the planning by engineers and the skills of the actual builders. He had been through this tunnel numerous times before, but never on a motorcycle. What if the frequency of the exhaust noise set up a resonance that caused the tunnel to collapse, despite its well-constructed arched structure? There were no vehicles coming out of the tunnel: what if a previous rider's bike had already collapsed the tunnel, causing a blockage that his bike would slam against?

He knew his own expertise with electrical installations might have inherent flaws that could come into play somewhere in the future. What if that future was now? What if one of the workers laying the rocks had had a momentary distraction one day that could lead to a flaw that could collapse the tunnel years later, exactly when he was riding through it? Could an external rockslide wipe out the power line at the same time his bike's headlight burned out, leaving him riding through total darkness to crash to sudden death? Had he stopped only to allow his ears to clear, or had these other subconscious thoughts exaggerated his fear of never emerging from the far side of the tunnel?

As Mark briefly contemplated these things, sitting there astride the Harley, were these trepidations of dying unexpectedly a result of the guilt he was feeling? The chances of any of those things happening was so small, it was absolutely ludicrous to even be thinking about it. Apparently he was just playing games with himself to forestall the inevitable conclusion that he was going to have to make some changes in his life. If he survived this ride, would he go home to Allison and apologize for his failures, or would his selfishness continue? Would he be able to tell his kids he loved them and regretted not making himself available at past crucial times in their lives, when a father's impact would have been most beneficial?

What if this realization had come so delayed that it would be too late for any reconciliation? He had been satisfied all these years with how his life had tracked at home. Even if he didn't have the guts to confess to his family, he couldn't go on living as before. Similarly, even if he didn't go through the tunnel, but turned around to go back the way he'd come, there was no way to avoid the conclusions that he'd reached.

Actually, he realized, he really did need to proceed through the tunnel, facing any unknowns that might complicate the completion of his journey. It was like a tunnel of fate. His ears had cleared, but his mind stayed cloudy. He revved the throttle, and the engine seemed to chortle. It was a sound that once had thrilled him, but now it chilled, as if evil had consumed his machine. His once perfect life was a travesty, and there was no one to blame but himself!

Getting his job at Addison had been such a stroke of good luck. He had been a real goof-off all through high school. He had never really tried for good grades, being satisfied to just get by. It had been fun, and more of a challenge, to play good practical jokes. Over time, as his classmates figured out his propensity in that regard, he had been required to be more and more innovative. Once they had become aware of his shenanigans, success was harder to achieve. He loved it, because when someone else wanted to play a trick on a friend (or foe), they'd come to Mark for assistance. His ploys had mostly been good-natured, but occasionally there had been pranks that had gone past innocence, so there had been some slight harm to people and property. However, he took consolation that those times had been tricks against prideful people, he now thought proudly. It had served them right, and according to his viewpoint, they had needed to be taken down a peg or two.

But again, now came that sudden revelation that the victims of his jokes had been selected strictly by his own criteria. Yet, what had given him any authority to decide the fate of who deserved such derision? He had been selfish all through his years at school and had never thought about it until just now! How? How could he have been so deceived? Why had none of his friends ever mentioned it? He thought he had been well liked, but what if all that time his "friends" had only pretended so that they wouldn't be the dupes of his ridiculous pranks? None of them had kept in contact with him over the years, so perhaps they really hated him. He had moved several hundred miles away, so that might be why, but who knew? He'd been a dunce back then and still was!

When he had seen the job advertisement by Addison Electric back then, he was desperately in need of cash and had spent every dime on a bus ticket to get to the interview. He'd had no credentials or prior experience, but he loved being outdoors. Addison needed another team member, a grunt/go-fer, to complete the contract for the power line installation. They needed someone who would be willing to be out in the bush for weeks at a time, so they took a chance on Mark. He was young and strong, and seemed willing to work.

He had carried bags of dry ready-mix concrete, and then the water to activate and set it, hundreds of yards from base camps to where poles needed to be anchored to the ground. Those poles had been brought to the sites by helicopters, and he had detached cables from the poles, fighting to stay standing on the mountain slope while the downwash from the rotor blades buffeted him with dust-laden high-velocity gusts. He was sure-footed and loved the adventures. With him, Addison had a dedicated employee, and there was absolutely no inclination for practical joking on such a demanding and exhausting job. Mark was converted from a boy to a man overnight.

Although Mark and the crew had worked in rain and in snow, they stayed in town during the most inclement weather. It was during one of those bouts of foul weather that Mark had met Allison. She was the niece of the Maggie who owned Maggie's Diner, waiting tables and booths to save up enough money to go to college. At least, that had been her plan at the time. It had been like a movie, when Mark had first entered the diner. Their eyes met, then locked for a few seconds, before Mark and his fellow crew members made their way to an empty table. It wasn't necessarily "love at first sight," but there was a mutual interest in a further pursuit of happiness.

Thereafter, every time the crew had any downtime, Mark had hung out at the diner. Allison was usually there, too, whether on the payroll or not. Maggie had concurred with the situation, and if at any time Mark made an unexpected appearance, she'd call to let Allison know. Maggie and Mark had become good friends, too. Even today, Maggie was still a good friend, he thought, though so frail she could die at any time. Before that happened, he really needed to apologize to her, too, for not being there when Uncle Frank had died, or when her appendix had burst, sending her to the hospital for a week. He was such a jerk!

After the contract for running the tunnel's power line had been completed ahead of schedule, all the crew members got a bonus. Addison had won several other local contracts, so they had offered Mark a permanent position. Mark had already saved much of his income from his first job, since the majority of his time spent in the bush meant there was less time to spend money. He and Allison had married when he took the full-time position with Addison. A few of Allison's friends and Mark's fellow crew members had been invited to the short-planned but inevitable event. Of course, Maggie and Frank had been there, too. Addison had given Mark a paid month off work, and the newlyweds had flown to Hawaii. It was the last time either of them ever left the valley again. Mark had worked only on those nearby contracts, but even they had kept him away from home much of the time. It was great income, but poor planning for a home life. He had never thought to take Allison on another excursion, or cruise, or vacation, or...anything. He was a mighty fine fool!

Allison had been such a good mother. She still was! As a testimony to that, all four of the kids still lived close-by. She provided the focal point for get-togethers and special family occasions. Much of the time, she had had to be both mother and father for not only the kids, but for the next generation, too. That meant he had missed out on so many things where two generations had grown up with only minimal assistance from him. He had missed out on his kids' sporting events, recitals, plays, broken arms, and lost puppies, and now he was missing those similar events of his grandchildren. He didn't even know if his own kids were being better parents than he had been, or if they had followed the example of a bad mentor. How foolish he had been!

Working for Addison had provided a great career, allowing him to gain experience in many diverse areas. He had used dynamite to blast away solid rocks where poles needed to be set. He had rappelled over sheer ledges with 120 pounds strapped to his back. He had rescued fellow crew members from crevasses and slippery slopes. He had climbed poles and strung conductive wires high above the landscape so they could remain clear of rock outcroppings above and below. He had used pneumatic drills with diamond bits to bore anchor holes for guy wire eye bolts. He had cooked thousands of meals over a backpack propane stove. He had used chips of stone in lieu of spoons and plates because water was too valuable to be wasted on washing dishes. He had drunk rainwater that had accumulated in pockets in the rock for the same reason. He had improvised repairs on all kinds of equipment so it would be able to last until they could return to civilization for proper repairs.

Mark had adapted well to the various demands needed to succeed in these kinds of projects. He had been promoted after less than ten years to lead a team of his own. He had earned quite a respectable income, and now owned outright his house and several hundred acres of valley land. He had acquired toys, like this Harley Davidson motorcycle, that gave him pleasure in his retirement years. But he had never counseled any of his younger crew members who had struggled to survive the lonely limitations of project work. He had never shared his experiences with ways to cope with loneliness until it was time to return to town. He had not shown any compassion when it was needed. Somehow, those needed interactions had escaped his attention, because he had been enclosed in his own personal world. How could he have been so blind?

Allison loved him deeply, he was sure. She had started calling him her "rugged man" early in their relationship, and still did today. She remained kind and affectionate after all these years and had never complained about his long absences. She was strong and independent, and had managed household affairs efficiently at all times, and he had never had to worry about her well-being while away. But he couldn't remember one time when he had returned and had asked about what had needed repairing while he was gone. He had not noticed there was a new roof on the house until two years later. It was like it had not ever occurred to Allison to mention household affairs any time he'd returned from an extended absence. Did she think it would have bugged him too much? Had she thought he just didn't care? Indeed, had he cared? He had just taken it all for granted, that she would handle things. All those years of their marriage, he had taken Allison for granted. What an imbecile he was.

Of course he had done a lot too, he justified in his mind. He had provided well, financially, and Allison had never had to work outside their homestead. After their family was grown, she had volunteered at church and community festivities. She knew everyone in town, and they knew her. But few knew her husband, whom they had seldom—or never—seen before. Already, since his retirement, there had been multiple times of embarrassment when he and Allison had been out and around town. People who were strangers to him were close associates of Allison's. A few had even admitted that they didn't realize that Allison was married. He was like an unnecessary accessory, just tagging along on her shirttails. Her life seemed so meaningful compared to his, with all of her friends and connections throughout the community. She was more successful than he was, and he had pretty much ignored that part of her life due to his own selfishness. He was really just a failure when it came to interrelationships with other people!

Although it had been less than ten minutes since Mark had pulled over to the side of the road in front of the tunnel, it seemed like he had just relived his entire life. Was that all he was worth, ten minutes of existence? Would he be able to compensate for any of his failures when he got back home? Could there be any restitution with his family members, especially Allison? He tried to visualize how various scenarios might play out once he got back to Vantage. With the kids so accustomed to his absences, how could anything he'd say or do make up for his lack of providing proper fatherly duties? Why had none of them challenged his lack of actions? Were the grandkids also already so matured that they would be unreachable?

And what of his absurd thoughts about imagined dangers inside tunnels that had occupied his mind just minutes before? There seemed to be absolutely no justification for those fears. Even if the tunnel had hidden dangers that could not be evaluated or corrected from the outside, there could be an eventual fix. Unfortunately, the turbulence and mysteries inside his own tunneled mind might not ever get resolved. There were strewn boulders everywhere inside his head, trying to block his newborn thoughts from clearing his mental passageways. The lights that had been out for so long finally had a slim glimmer. Could he find the extra resources needed to fully brighten the interior darkness that he had kept restricted by pure selfishness?

Could he string mental wires in the correct order and directions to make connections he couldn't even fully visualize? Could he, the ultimate buffoon, untangle the massive injustices he had caused by his negligence? Could the vectors that he had twisted into his own self-centered perspectives be redirected towards helping others, especially

Allison and his family, find him to be a more acceptable person? He knew he couldn't blast his way in, but might he be able to slowly chisel and chip away his hard covering of ego-rock? He slipped the Harley into gear and eased it across the gravel to the pavement. It was time to find out.

A Southern Gentle Man
Excerpts from the Biography of Jodie Barton

Laura Hunter

The Beginning

Ancient Egyptians believed man's immortality is more secure each time his name is spoken. This belief forced them to chisel away any reference to a pharaoh they wanted to annihilate from history and from his afterlife. If their maxim is true, Jodie Barton transcends death. His name is spoken.

There are those who would say a man's life begins the day he is born and ends with his last breath. Not so with Jodie Barton. These years later, I, his oldest daughter, am recognized, not for my identity today, but in Walker County, Alabama, by the fact that I am his daughter.

Here was a man whose parents had wanted a son even before his conception, a man whose personality and integrity live beyond him these five decades after his death.

Like others of the time, the family scrapped by, eating what could be grown or what could be gathered or killed in the woods. My father worked for almost half a century. He never tried to finish school. Life was easier for the family because the mother and father could read and write, as could my father. He manipulated math problems as quickly as they could be rattled off. And musical talent ran through his veins thicker than burnt motor oil he used to cure mange on his hunting dogs.

***

The summer before he was to begin first grade, his father, Papa, was teaching Daddy the art of whittling, a pastime common to males of the day. Like most adults have to do with children, Papa told him what to do again and again: "Slice the wood with the knife blade *away* from your body."

Daddy, like many kids, did it his way. In one swoop, he turned the knife toward his face. One heavy draw of his right hand into soft wood, and the knife slipped. It sliced open his left eyeball, leaving it intact, but blind.

Cutting his eyeball through gave him respect for knives, but his respect never turned to fear. He forever had his pocketknife handy and used it to cut chunks off apples he grew in the yard, as he sat in the yard swing, resting from work or gardening. The accident took a year away from his starting school and gave his mother additional time to convince Papa that she needed to cut Daddy's white curls, curls that had never seen scissors come near. Most of the time, he wore one long braid to his waist, much like that of an old woodsman. Perhaps because of his youth at the time of the accident, perhaps because of his determination, the blindness never hampered his success.

But Fate favored him. In his late teens or early twenties, he was riding a truck's running board, driver's side, when the truck met an on-coming truck with a piece of wood, or a log, tied to the top. The wood slammed into his face and scooped out an eye. The hit took the blinded eye. In time he was able to afford a glass eye to fill in the hole. Each night for the rest of his life, he removed the eye, gently washed it and dropped it for safe keeping into a glass of water by the bed. Each morning, he dried the eye with a clean handkerchief and slipped it back in place. Eventually, because there was no muscle to hold the eye secure, the glass eye sunk deeper into its hole.

No one ever mentioned the sunken eye socket. Courtesy common to the day held people's tongues. Or perhaps it was a time when war-damaged bodies were the norm, a time when physical image counted for less.

When the world set about killing itself off, the lost eye kept him from both World Wars. Most males were drafted or had enlisted. Women who held a secondary role in society found themselves stranded. Graduates of Cordova High School in 1945 numbered forty-two females and ten males. Most of the community's males had attended summer school or dropped out before graduation so they could enlist. My father showed to the community left at home, most with no males about, what a gentle man can be. Those qualities established his reputation and remained with him throughout his life.

The Changing

My father lies under the hill where the old home place stood on Lynn's Park Road, across what is now State Highway

78, across from Black Water where he played and swam as a child. At some prior time, he and my mother had to have selected the burial site, for it is a good one.

My great-great-great-great-grandfather Moses Barton had given the land for the cemetery to anyone who wanted to be buried there, free, with the understanding that family would have first plot choice. Family can no longer be buried there. No plots in the original site remain.

***

There are those who say they kept our children, who were less than two, during the funeral and burial. So many have told me that, that were it all true, a flock of cluckers would have hovered over both. I don't know the answer to who or how many. I was lost, totally and completely, so lost I put those days out of my mind for years.

What I remember each time I walk up that hill to his grave begins with seeing a group of men encircling a green-draped hole. I knew that Daddy's nephew Sidney and Autry Reed had asked to dig the grave. I knew they had to use pickaxes to break through Alabama shale and clay.

These men were different. They were not Sidney or Autry. These men leaned on their long-handled shovels, waiting to cover my daddy with the dirt. When gravediggers appear at any burial now, that day washes over me like muddy water.

The funeral directors had set folding chairs covered in green felt under a green tent. The ground was covered with fake green carpet. Synthetic green carpet covered the mound of orange clay off to one side.

What is it with these green coverings? Are those who are in the business of the dead and bereaved trying to make us who are left behind believe that green grass sprouts miraculously out of Alabama red clay?

Someone needs to tell them that no miracle lies there. The miracle lies in the living memories of those they seal up in concrete vaults and cover with soil. These memories cannot be buried. They emerge on their own. The miracle lies in the fact that those memories will never be secreted, as long as a man's name, as the Egyptians believed, is spoken.

***

Four of us walked up the hill that day. Tom and me, followed by my mother and sister. Tom sat on the end, nearest the road. He put me between himself and my mother. My sister sat on our mother's left.

The preacher said whatever it is preachers say standing at the edge of the tent. I didn't hear him. I watched the coffin, waiting for its weight to split the 2x6s that straddled the hole, waiting for it to fall, catawampus into the ground, standing my daddy on his head.

I'm sure the red oaks throughout the cemetery reflected diffused light with their reds, oranges, their browning leaves. They do each fall. I am sure the monster cedar greens were black with age. They are today. I didn't notice. I sat mesmerized. The greenness had been bought from the funeral home. Their decoration created its own aura.

I didn't hear anyone. I didn't see anything but green. Then I looked at the coffin lid. The longer I looked, the more convinced I was that it was not closed.

I whispered to Tom. "The coffin's not closed." He didn't answer me.

I whispered to Mama. "The lid's open." She said nothing.

She patted my knee, for she had known, perhaps for years, this day would be bad for me.

Neither listened to me. They shushed me.

I called out to anyone who would listen, first softly. Then louder.

"The coffin's not locked," I said.

The longer I waited for someone to respond the more frantic I became.

I begged someone to check it. I spoke louder and louder, then over the voice of the preacher. I rose, stepping over the corner of the hole, and went to the funeral director who stood to one side, Tom tugging me back. I said to the director's face, "The coffin's not closed."

He insisted the lid was closed. And locked. He had done it himself. He lied. Yes. He lied. Was the issue of the coffin lid a vision? An omen? Call it what you will. It dances even now, a demon spinning inside my head.

It was then someone pulled me away, moving me down the hill. Hysterical, I tried to shake hands off my arms. My father needed me to get back up the hill. To stop this travesty.

I pleaded for them not to do this to my daddy.

People stepped back, uncertain of what to do with me. Those who were not scared of me tried to console me. My husband, not knowing what to do, let my former sweetheart talk to me, thinking he might get through.

No talking, no touching, nothing changed the reality of that moment, the moment I realized they were lowering an open coffin into the ground and my daddy was in it.

Someone put me in a car and took me away. When they brought me back, faceless men with shovels had smothered my daddy with dirt.

Today backhoes work faster than men with shovels. Yellow machines wait in the background, pretending to be invisible, until someone moves them forward to shove dirt into the grave. Their mechanical oily funeral smell reeks more strongly of inhumanity than the odor of dirt ever did.

At home, neighbors swaged tables and counters with heavy bowls and platters of food. It would have been better had I eaten, chewed the grief, rather than swallow it whole.

Everyone told me he was gone. And he was for a few days.

Then one afternoon as I drove home from work, he appeared in the passenger's seat next to me. He was so real the car smelled of Old Spice and warm yeast rising.

"Don't worry, Hot Shot. It's all right," he said.

He drove home with me every day for the remainder of that year. We talked; me aloud, him silently. Then he moved into some spare room in my psyche. "It's all right."

***

My mother attended Eastern Star meetings in town one Tuesday night out of the month. Daddy, my sister and I would go to the Dixie Theater in Cordova to see a movie while she went to her meeting. My ticket cost a dime. A dime movie trip with Daddy meant a grand time.

About 1950, when televisions first appeared on the market, the owner of the Dixie Theater lured people in with the promise of drawing for a new television set, an elite prize for the day. A crowd lined the sidewalk, worming its way to the ticket booth then wadding itself into groups waiting for the doors to open.

Blacks paid for their tickets after the whites finished.

They entered a door on the left to climb to the balcony. No one stood to take their ticket stubs for the drawing.

Daddy bought our tickets. We handed our tickets to a dark-suited man inside the right-hand door. The man tore the tickets in two and dropped the stub of each into a box as we entered.

After the movie, velvet curtains closed off the screen, and the town Mayor, who was also the movie theater owner, came on stage with the box of ticket stubs.

The winner of the first drawing must have left early. No one claimed the number. So the Mayor drew again.

He drew *my* number. I could not believe it. A television set. All my own. The only person I knew who had a television set was our neighbor, Larry Dempsey, and my sister and I thought Larry had everything he wanted.

It was dim in the theater, so I asked Daddy to check my stub. Daddy checked all three of our ticket stubs. The Mayor *had* called my number.

Daddy led both of us girls up on the stage and handed the Mayor my ticket stub. He said something along the line of "Well, here's our big winner" and started to shake Daddy's hand.

"No. It's her ticket," Daddy said and pushed me up in front of him.

Mayor stuttered. "She can't win. She ain't got no adult ticket."

Daddy's back stiffened. "Nobody said it had to be an adult ticket. If she couldn't win, you shouldn't have put her ticket in the box. You took her ticket yourself when we came in."

I was getting a bit antsy. I had never heard Daddy argue with anybody before.

"Well, she can't have the television. She's a kid." No apology. No nothing. Just a flat refusal.

Someone in the audience called out, "Let the kid have the television." Others came out with calls like, "Yeah, give it to her."

The Mayor did not budge. He reached in to draw another winner. The crowd settled in, quiet now, listening. He might draw their ticket this time.

The three of us left the stage and walked down the aisle between the rest of the movie-goers, everyone waiting to get my television set.

Outside, I asked Daddy why he did not just let the Mayor think the ticket was his.

"It wasn't my ticket. That's why."

The television incident taught me much about people. There are people who will take from a child without conscience. More importantly, there are people who cannot lie, even to appease a child.

Daddy bought us a television set in 1953 so we could watch the coronation of Elizabeth II. It was a good television for its day. It arrived in June, so we had the entire summer to learn who Lucy and Ethel and Roy and Dale and Gene Autry were. We gloried in the Golden Age of Cowboy Westerns.

Mama bought Daddy an avocado green wing-back chair to set by his bed. Winter nights he sat in his chair while Jodie Lynne and I sat on the bed like Indian braves around the tepee fire, watching programs interrupted with lines of white dots rolling top to bottom, white dots we called "snow."

In the next bedroom, Mama sewed on into the night for some client, bringing in a little extra money to cover the chair.

The Breadman

Most of Daddy's life was spent delivering. He worked in Virginia delivering bread with his uncle John McCrary, Sr. and Sons, who owned the Honey Krust Bread and Cakes franchise. Back in Alabama, he butchered for a short time at Cottons Mercantile and sometimes delivered grocery orders to housewives who had no way to get their orders themselves.

During WWII, because he was 4-F, he delivered vegetables house to house and sold them out of the back of a battered pickup.

War rationing hit the homeland people in the belly. Color-coded stamps and food coupons began in 1942, the year I was born. It moved on to "Sugar Buying Cards" in 1943. Then tires. Access to tires depended on a worker's distance to a job and the job's importance to the war effort. If the right connections were met, tires could be bought through the black market. After tire rationing came gasoline. Rural people, like my family, were left to gardening and walking.

When Daddy could get no more ration coupons for tires, he parked the truck under a colossal cedar tree in the front yard and left it there.

For years, the severe contrast between a rusting truck and the brilliant white of a cedar trunk, swabbed each spring with a mixture of lime and water, marked the distance between wanting to do better and being able to.

Daddy held his longest job delivering bread for Ward Bread Company: Tip-Top. He drove with one blind eye more than twenty-five years with a perfect record. His driving record allowed him to select premiums each year. By the time he retired because of his health, both my sister and I had a full set of sterling silverware, as well as coffee and tea services that sit on silver trays.

***

I was the summer helper. Truth be known, it was probably against company policy to let some scrawny kid ride in the truck, but I went faithfully. Most of the time, I rode sitting on the top step, where the open folding bus-type door caught some passing air. I kept one arm wrapped around the metal rod used for hoisting up into the truck. This rod was my safety guarantee. I believed as long as I held to the bar I could not get dumped out on the road. The flaw in that logic never occurred to me. Sometimes I rode, the wind in my face, standing behind Daddy as he drove.

I knew every stop, every owner, almost every customer in each little Walker County country store. I learned how much bread this store would sell during the weekend, how many packages of hamburger buns to add if a holiday was coming up, who preferred devil's food cakes over raisin cakes, and who would give orders for fruitcakes in Wedgewood colored tins, embossed in cream-colored Grecian ladies, for Thanksgiving and Christmas. After I qualified for a drivers' license, I delivered the Paradise fruit cakes to homes, to cut Daddy's hours.

I was a jump-and-run worker. Every minute I delayed meant we would get home later, and Daddy would have less time to rest. I ate what Daddy called my "pay," a fried ham sandwich and Orange Crush "dope," at Short's Café in Cordova.

***

Daddy had to be at the warehouse we called the "bread barn" every morning except Saturdays and Sundays at 4:00 to meet the delivery truck from the Birmingham bakery. He checked his order to see that what he had ordered the day before matched what had been sent. Then he loaded the truck with the day's deliveries.

Days were long. Three days each week, he delivered into Cullman County. On those days, Monday, Wednesday, Friday, his workday started at 4:00 a.m. and ended, if early, by 9:00 p.m. Such a schedule lends itself to seeking help. He carried my sister, and almost all my cousins, at least once.

Some might say he wanted the help. I know better. He took the kids because he realized that a day on the bread truck would be open to adventures, good and bad.

Ah, yes. The day of the fox. One of the best.

Red fox, even during the 1950s, stayed out of sight because so few were left in the wild. Even hunters refused to let a red fox be killed.

This day as Daddy drove down a dirt road to some out-of-the-way store, a red fox, his feathery tail tinged in orange, trotted out of the woods along the road. He took his time, accessing that this area was still his domain.

Daddy braked, and we watched, whispering as if the fox now standing in the middle of the road could hear what we said. The fox turned his pointy nose and his sharp ears straight toward us. Once he decided we were no threat, he took up his mission and moved on across the road. His dignified movements, his upright head, announced to the woods, and to us, that here was his realm.

I stood breathless. I had never seen a fox up close, certainly not a red fox. This fox was magnificent, so colorful I cannot imagine how he could camouflage himself in the woods. His stately moves, his proportioned body with its thin legs, its tail the length of its body, set him apart from any canine I have ever seen.

***

My sister rode the truck, but she preferred to avoid Barney, a coal mining camp south of Cordova. A Black man with no legs owned a small general store there. This man rolled himself around the store in a straight-backed chair to which he had attached wheels. He had rigged a device so he could open the door from behind the low counter, if someone needed help coming in.

The door opened without a touch as Daddy, and Jodie Lynne or I, approached to check bread supplies. Then the door opened again, seemingly on its own, when we came back with arms stacked just right so the loaves would not squish themselves by their freshness.

My sister maintains she was afraid.

Of what? The supernatural door? The darkness of the little store, its only opening the magical door with framed windows across the top half? The Black man himself because he had no legs? The Black man because he was black?

Her fear could have generated from one, or all. We knew no Black people. To me, he was a curiosity. He had taken a simple chair and made it move. He was a wonder.

But Daddy tired to dissipate her fear each time, before they entered into that world she knew nothing about.

Those days taught responsibility in a positive way. Each day taught the importance of courtesy. It taught us children on that one day, as on any other day, that respect can extend beyond those closest to them.

***

Me?

He took me to keep me out of trouble. I was a saucy child. My sassiness riled my mother if I was left alone with her too long. My contesting whys would lift the hair on the back of her neck as surely as if she had been plugged into an electrical socket.

She grew into a meticulous person who needed everything just so. I needed freedom. There lived within me a spirit fighting to fly, to break out and experience all life had to offer, even if it involved risks.

I worked the route more often than any of the other kids.

At the end of the workday, Daddy would write out an order for the coming day: how many loaves of bread, how many packages of hamburger and hotdog buns, how many little round raisin cakes, how many little layered devils food cakes, in November and December, how many Paradise fruitcakes.

He counted his money and recorded the total. Then he added the totals he had recorded at each store that day. He wrote out four and five-digit numbers in a single column. He simply looked down the list of collections and put the total at the bottom of a two-to-three-page list. He never erased, nor did he re-tally. It was as if the numbers added themselves in his mind.

I thought he was magic. He took this skill for granted, assuming anyone could do it.

Not me. I stood amazed.

Before we could leave the bread barn, the truck had to be unloaded. All the empty wooden bread boxes, all the items we had picked up because they had not sold, went back into the barn. Emptying the truck was the dirtiest chore of the day, for we had ridden mile after mile down a day's worth of dirt roads, collecting dust that swirled in the front door, settled on us, with only a smattering blowing out the back.

While Daddy tallied, I swept out the truck. I arrived home with black rings around my fingernails, a face smeared with dirt, an occasional spider bite on a leg or arm, a bruise here and there, clothes that had to be bleached, and gummy white hair. But having my father to myself for that day was worth every grungy bit I gathered.

The development of adding machines, then calculators, saved me from the fact that I cannot work math; and after decades of teaching writing and spelling, I still cannot spell *chrysanthemum*. But he could. He would tease me when I stumbled over the letters as if they were bruising gravel under bare feet.

Daddy drove with one eye. Unlike me, he added without counting on his fingers.

He pleasured friends and strangers alike with a finger salute to his cap and a "Tip Top," when asked him how he was doing.

For Walker and part of Cullman Counties, Jodie Barton was *the* bread man.

The Dogman

My father was a highly respected dogman. A dogman is a hunter who values his dogs more than he values the hunt. He values the sound of baying and yowling, at treeing coons or ousting rabbits more than he values spilling blood. Most often on his hunts, prey is released, and the dogs brought home to their regular diet.

Only a true dogman understands the ethics of another dogman. The dogman places an identification collar on each of his dogs. Anyone who finds that dog feeds and cares for the dog as if it were his own, until he can get the dog back to its owner.

***

The only time I heard my father speak disrespectfully of another person was the time one of my elementary school classmates, who grew up to call himself a "dogman," "a rabbit hunter," stole a black and tan beagle.

The beagle was not the best dog in the pack, but it did belong to my father. And it did have Daddy's collar around its neck. For a dogman, to keep is to steal.

Dogmen throughout the county knew the beagle was missing. They searched for the dog each time they hunted. It never came when Daddy blew his identifying call on the sculpted cow's horn he trained his pack to answer to. All good hunting dogs, whether fox hound or beagle, come when they hear the distinctive voice of their owner's horn. The dog never answered. It was either dead or chained somewhere.

***

After several months, the thief must have thought the dog was forgotten, because he took it on a hunt. An authentic dogman can recognize, even several miles away, the voice of each dog, even if it is not his own. He knows every dog's song.

My father was not on this hunt for some unremembered reason. But by the next day's end, he knew who had his dog.

Sunday afternoon, refusing to let me go along, though I argued that I knew the thief, he drove to the guy's house and confronted him. I learned details at supper.

***

"I've come for my dog," he said.

Of course, he denied having the dog, but Daddy would not accept the denial.

"I walked straight to the dog pen," Daddy told me later, "pointed to the dog, and said, 'That's my dog there. Get her out.'"

She was Daddy's dog. She still wore his collar.

In the 1950s such could be grounds for an arrest, a fist fight, or a shoot-out. My father chose none of these.

"Open the pen," he said.

The guy did.

Daddy whistled for the dog and walked away, his dog following at his heels. He opened the door to the wooden box he had built for the back of the dog truck. She jumped up on the tailgate and trotted in. Daddy shut the windowed gate and drove away.

***

Such actions shamed the young man more than any whipping. He realized other dogmen knew of his deceit. He dropped out of sight. Perhaps he hunted somewhere else. Perhaps he never hunted again.

I knew the integrity of a dogman. This guy was no dogman. I was so angry at what he had done I did not care if he had a chance to hunt again. My daddy had his dog back. Pride puffed my chest with knowing he had recovered her in a gentlemanly manner.

What he had to say about the thief, he said at home. That is the only time I ever heard his anger provoke him to call another person "sorry."

***

The dogmen gathered each Saturday night at someone's house, agreed on a hunt site and set out together. Deep within the woods they built a fire, if weather called for it, or they sat around in a circle, just talking low, waiting for the first dog to hit a trail, to pick up a scent.

Whatever the conversation within the group, the topic would be interrupted. "There goes Jack." "Ole Bess' got the scent." "Looks like Sally's pup is gonna be a good one." Butt-ins were expected, never opposed.

Most of the men never moved from that site, unless they had to follow a dog and pull it off its prey. The dogs preferred blood. The men preferred camaraderie, the bond darkness afforded with nature and with each other.

***

Their bond was a lifelong commitment. When my father died, dogmen brought food to the house after he had been buried, because they knew that my mother had little income. From time to time, she would find sacks filled with groceries on the back porch.

Dogman Carl Phifer bought my daddy's old dog truck and his dog trailer. My husband Tom remembers the truck and a dog Phifer got.

Though the bitch was old, Daddy had kept her. "The best dog I ever had," he told Tom.

The truck was dark, possibly green, rusted, and used only for hunts. A 1953 Chevrolet still running in 1967, with a floor starter under the right foot, the truck rattled about on logging and dirt roads to and from a night's hunt. It was in such bad repair it would not have gone much farther. The dog crate in the back protected the dogs from rain, wind and cold. Their safety mattered more than the truck's condition.

Phifer did not need what he bought. He bought them simply because they had belonged to Jodie Barton.

After the burial, Phifer came one evening before dusk with $300 in hand. He gave the money to my mother because he said he knew what one of the dogs she had given him was worth. He had been with my daddy when he bought the dog, he told her. In 1968, $300 was a wealth of money. There was no way my father could have paid $300 for a dog. The money was the dogman's gesture of respect for my father.

My mother gave Daddy's pack to Vic Handley to sell for her because she needed money. At his death, Daddy had thirty-six beagles, thirty-six of the finest, healthiest beagles in Walker County.

***

As children, I, like most of my cousins, was allowed to go on hunts. The boys, Sidney and, years later, Mike, were allowed to stay out later than I was. As I grew older, I gave up on the hunts. The dogmen did not talk about much I was interested in. I could not tell one dog from another, unless I saw the dog in the light. I never learned their songs. And midnight comes early for little girls.

Years later, Daddy and I walked the woods in our own form of hunt, listening to his beagles. Doing nothing special, just meandering and talking. Just him and me, walking the woods.

As a young man, my father hunted fox. His delight lay in his pack, but he often had a stud or bitch that stood out from the others. These he took to judgings and with them brought home ribbons and honors.

One dog, Sprugeon Wheeler, won first place in the Alabama Bench Show competition. Daddy stood with Wheeler, #1 in what would today be the equivalent of AKC Best of Show. I do not remember the dog, but I do remember the pride each time Daddy took out the magazine to look at the photograph.

***

Sidney, Daddy's nephew who saw his uncle as a second father, went fox hunting. Being male, though he started the hunt a tired boy, he refused to sleep because he feared he would let his "Unka Jodie" down. Sidney remembers being impressed by the fact that his uncle could tell by the dogs' voices when a fox had been cornered. Learning the language of the dogs took time and patience. This "singing" produced a language that resonated between man and animal, a language that set the dogman apart from the average person.

***

A self-taught veterinarian, Daddy kept a veterinarian's medical book stored away so he could cure mange with a dip into sulfur and burnt motor oil, help deliver pups for a bitch having a difficult labor, handle snake bites on legs and curious noses, whatever overcame his pack.

Within Daddy's notebook is a treatment for curing black tongue, a disease caused by lack of niacin. Its first symptoms appear in the mouth. The book also contains a cure for mange, a highly contagious skin disease. Daddy always kept a tub of mange treatment at the ready.

He never hesitated to share his information with other hunters: "For Curing Mange: 'One quart motor oil, two tablespoonfuls turpentine, one teaspoonful carbolic acid, one quart of coal oil, one pound sulfur, one box Dr. Hess' Healing Powder. Mix well and put on with a small paint brush.'"

Daddy followed the treatment exactly until he hit the last order. He did not paint his dogs. To do so would be too time consuming. He just grabbed the dog by the scruff of the neck and dipped him into the tub of chemicals. Daddy kept an eye to his dogs, so rarely did a dog need a second dipping.

No dogs were better cared for than his. Everyone in the family comments on how he tended his dogs. They had their own special diet. He poured melted lard over their "dog bread," a filler for dry food, to keep coats slick and shiny. Each day our mother baked dog bread by mixing cornmeal and lard with water. She cooked the mixture in a sixteen-inch iron skillet and dumped it, bottom up, to cool. Everybody, family or friend, who walked past the platter of bread pone took a pinch off the crusty side or bottom. If supper was late and several nibbling people passed through the kitchen, the dogs might not get any crust at all.

***

Feeding the dogs had its own routine: Crumble dog bread and mix with dry food. Pour several cups of melted lard over the mixture at least once a week. Moisten mixture with water. Dump the dog food into pans on the ground and back away, before a bitch knocks you down getting to her supper.

All our dogs ate the same dog food. They flourished. If a dog managed to kill on the hunt, she was not allowed to eat the prey. And no one considered *ever* offering a dog scraps from the kitchen table. Not when Daddy's recipe worked so well.

***

Every spring Daddy inoculated each dog against rabies, a disease most people referred to as "the hydrophobie." Any dog bit on a hunt could be infected by a rabid coon or fox. "The hydrophobie" is deadly for any mammal, including people. Keeping disease out of the dog pen was critical. One shot per dog each year kept rabies at bay.

Daddy trained me in holding a dog's muzzle so the dog could take the shot without biting the owner or his assistant— me. The trick is to wrap the right arm around the dog's neck so she will be soothed yet held in place. The safety tip is to clinch the dog's muzzle, gently but firmly, between the eyes and nose so she cannot bite. To squeeze too tight will frighten her, and she will fight against the hold. With both arm and hand in place, the holder and the shooter are protected. The dog cannot squirm and cause the needle to inflict more pain, for hypodermics in the 1950s and 1960s resembled hollow ten-penny nails more so than needles.

***

For some reason, one spring I was not handy when inoculations began in the side yard. When I arrived, Daddy had Mama holding the beagle chosen to be first. Only one dog at a time was taken from the pen. Hounds or beagles never ran free.

I drove into the yard, remembering not to park under the mulberry tree. I knew as soon as I saw Mama's stance, she was in trouble.

As I stepped out of the car, Daddy told her to move. She moved and released the muzzle just as Daddy injected the skin he had lifted off the dog's hip.

Daddy stuck. Mama howled. Louder than the dog, she howled.

The dog had bitten deep into the muscle of her left buttocks. She released the dog. The beagle ran yapping toward the well. Mama hobbled to the house, crying.

I could not blame her. Since having had a dog bite or two myself, I know how intense the pain is. I know how long it takes punctures to heal. The scars are not pretty, even if they are hidden under clothes. I understand why she sat on one side of her butt for almost a month.

I held all the dogs after that.

***

As I grew older, Daddy let his fox hounds go and centered on quality beagles, or "rabbit dogs." These short-legged black and tan dogs were just the right size for toting around. I could be found any day, as could my sister, with a pup or two in our arms.

One of my more serious infractions, according to my

mother's rules, occurred one winter night when I smuggled my beagle pup Little Man into the house. Worse still, I smuggled him into my bed, hiding him and his ultra-long, non-beagle ears between flannel sheets.

Before sneaking him in, I had not considered that beagle pups come into the world wiggling and yipping and scurrying about. Little Man managed all three as soon as I covered his head. Mama was in my room before I could get Little Man back under the covers. She took no mercy on the pup when I begged that he stay and that he would be cold outside. She argued that the pup would be warmer with his mother.

She saw a sheet layered with fleas, fleas hopping all over her house, and a puddle of dog pee seeping into her mattress. I saw a snuggly, furry bundle against my belly, keeping me warm throughout the night.

During the chaos, Daddy opened their bedroom door. Out popped his head, his glasses balanced on his nose, his hollow eye socket shut, clad in his Fruit of the Loom ribbed, sleeveless undershirt.

I saw that face and knew my time with Little Man in the house was over. We did not wake Daddy on a work night.

"Best mind your mother," he said and closed the door. Issue resolved.

We did not have dogs in the house. And we did.

I have seen Daddy bring in a bitch during cold or rain if she had difficult labor. He would put her on an old quilt next to the coal burning Thermadore heater in the center room of the house. As he delivered each pup, he would wipe it off and give it to Mama, who in turn, carried it to the kitchen, wrapped it with a washcloth and placed it on a towel on the open oven door for warmth. In the kitchen, mind you. On the oven door.

With this memory intact, I saw no harm in bringing in Little Man for company.

***

Daddy used his dogman expertise to teach me a strong emotional lesson when I was in high school. I wanted a cat. He said every time I asked, "Cats and dogs can't live on the same place."

I insisted I would not let anything happen to the cat. He told me to get a cat for the barn. I wanted a yard cat. I, who knew all, nagged until he agreed, leaving me with full responsibility when something happened to the cat.

It would be just a matter of time, I told myself. Let the dogs, *all* the dogs, the yard dogs and the beagles, get accustomed to having a cat in the yard, and the dogs would come around. My strategy would work. I meant it to.

My theory had more holes than a dry sponge. It did not take two weeks before I learned my lesson. One week-day night, yard dogs cornered the cat under the house where no one could save it. I had to sit inside and listen as dogs tore the cat to pieces under the floor.

And the commotion woke Daddy up. Again, on a work night.

I live with sentencing that cat to a horrific, needless death. The caterwauling and barking, the growling and screeching are all here, in my mind. Each time I hear a cat in distress I remember Daddy saying, "Cats and dogs can't live on the same place," and I check to see where the dog is.

***

Daddy always saw that my sister and I had a dog of our own. We each had a yard dog, and we could claim a beagle pup, as long as we did not let a good hunter get loose when we opened the pen. Once the pup reached hunt size, we had to give it up for another pup. We wagged puppies around each time a new litter came in.

My first dog arrived right after I was born. A dogman brought a russet chow pup with a tongue the color of midnight and put it down on the porch. The dog became mine. I later called him Mickey, after Mickey Mouse. When I was six, Daddy found him dead in sage brush down the hill. Poisoned.

I was a dogman myself, though I didn't know a girl could be a dogman. After Mickey died, I had to have another dog. After my second dog, I had to have another dog, but I, a wife now, lived in town. I did not marry a dogman, so I got a goldfish.

It would be years before I had another dog, a golden cocker given me by my daughter Michelle. The emptiness of not having a dog of my own all those years convinced me I had been a dogman all my life.

Swinging puppies was one of our favorite pastimes. Like babies, they cuddled and nuzzled into little balls, little balls with tails, and soon fell asleep. Once a pup slept, neither of us would dare wake it so we could shell butterbeans or shuck corn. Mama should know the pup needed his rest.

My second dog, a Boston terrier, I named Tags, after a dog in my first-grade reader. A classic black and white, she had one pup, a brown brindle with a crooked back leg. My sister took the pup and made it hers.

Tags lived eighteen years. Eventually so blind, she hid under the wooden steps, only to reach out and nip a neighbor on the ankle one day. Putting her down, as some owners do today, was never a consideration. She lived out her life with extra petting and comfort because she was family.

***

Owning a dog meant caring for the dog. Daddy cared for his. We cared for ours. Truth be known, Daddy had little use for yard dogs. They were there to placate my sister and me. He once went so far as to bring home a collie. A big dog.

This collie initiated a road trip one Sunday afternoon. Jodie Lynne remembers the trip as being one to North Alabama. With speed limits what they were (25-35 mph) and afternoons after church as short as they were before church began again, I imagine the trip never made it even close to the Tennessee state line. Maybe we made it to the next county.

We all climbed in the Chevrolet. I know the car had to be a Chevy. Daddy believed in Chevys, except once when he ventured out and bought a maroon Mercury Comet. This trip, however, was a pre-Comet trip.

The collie's name was Lassie, of course. Daddy called her "a beaut," beautiful enough to star on television. When she disappeared, Daddy suspected she had been stolen. My sister's grief sent Daddy and his dogmen on a search everywhere, asking everyone to look for her.

Someone told Daddy where to find her, at a farm, north, where an old couple lived. We picked her up that Sunday afternoon.

Lassie did not last long. When she started trying to bite anyone who came into her territory, her time grew short.

So. We brought Lassie home. Lassie bit Mama. Lassie left. In that order.

***

Now Jodie Lynne was dog-less.

Daddy surprised her one night when he came in from work. There inside his jacket was a blond Pekinese puppy. Jodie Lynne named her Cindy, but most people in the community knew her as "The World's Dumbest Dog." This dog imagined herself to be a ferocious beast bent on protecting her territory.

She would chase any dog, German shepherds included, across the yard, until they turned on her. Then she dashed away in the opposite direction. But she picked up chase again as soon as the other dogs' backs were turned.

Cindy has the family-dog distinction of being the only dog who managed to be hit three different times by cars coming up the drive. She sat steadfast in the middle of the road and barked at cars until they got right to her. She would move out a bit, then dart back in front of the car, right under a wheel. She survived every hit.

Her pups were not so fortunate. The fortune teller got them. In a way.

Daddy allowed Cindy to be bred with the understanding that her pups be sold. Jodie Lynne squelched that plan. She went to the fortune teller.

Daddy had always told us never to go to a fortune teller. Fortune tellers went against the Bible.

The closest fortune teller lived in Parrish. That night Jodie Lynne drove to Parrish with a group of friends to try out the prophetess' wiles.

Back home, when Jodie Lynne drove into the carport, I yelled at her to stop. She had mashed one of Cindy's puppies. Instead of stopping, she backed out to miss the pup, not realizing that she had already killed it. As she backed away, she smashed the other puppies.

No puppies left to sell.

Jodie Lynne never told Mama or Daddy where she had been. But she has always felt that, if she had obeyed and stayed away from the fortune teller, she would not have killed Cindy's puppies.

***

I brought in stragglers of all kinds. I once picked up a sick, mangy dog outside Jasper and brought it home for Daddy to fix. I found the dog hobbling down the road in a dark winter rain. I had every faith Daddy could make the dog healthy. He kept his dogs at their best. Why not this one?

He told me the dog would not live. I felt that, if I wanted it to live hard enough, it would. I sat up all night with the dog in what we called the heater hall, the center room where the large coal-burning stove sat. The dog died before morning.

Daddy had made no attempt to heal the dog. The next morning Mama told me Daddy said as soon as he saw it that it had distemper. She reprimanded me for bringing in a stray and putting Daddy's dogs at risk. My attempt at apology was a weak "I didn't know." I was old enough to know better, she said.

I was. I was driving. I knew distemper is fatal. I had never seen a dog with distemper. Daddy's dogs just did not get distemper. His care kept them healthy. I had brought the dog in because I believed in the power of my father. Guilt over endangering his dogs washed over me in a torrent that continued for weeks.

Daddy buried the dog when he came home from work. He never mentioned the distemper.

***

They were not a demonstrative couple, my mother and father. I never remember hearing him tell my mother he loved her. The two of them did not show affection in public. No adults whispered, touched, giggled, kissed as I grew up. And, as the country song says, no one even guessed at what went on behind a closed door. Public Displays of Affection would have been scandalous.

I never remember him telling me he loved me. He did not have to. His love for me poured from his eyes and from a hand on my shoulder more assuredly than if he had spoken aloud.

One night when I was in the eleventh grade and leaving the next morning for an honors' convention in Birmingham, he came into the bedroom and, thinking I was asleep, kissed my cheek. I did not move, for fear of embarrassing him.

I never mentioned it to him. I think he would have been uncomfortable. I would not trade that peck on the cheek for a daily kiss that meant much less. I realize now I should have opened my eyes and said, "I love you, Daddy." I never did.

Nomenclature

Jennifer Horne

As a boy, you picked peaches.
Had enough of outdoor work.
No gardener, you developed
your own plant-naming system
based on color:
yellalias,
purpulias,
blueinnias,
oranganias.

Law school Latin
might have schooled you
for genus, species,
Linnaean nomenclature, but
you resisted classification.
You had so many names—
Allan, Al, Dick, Coach, Judge—
your self the same beneath each,
easy smile, solid core.

I knew you by another name,
the one that stays. The name I'd call
when you came in the door
from work, putting the day aside
with your hat and briefcase,
letting us shout
our welcomes, our relief
at your reliable reappearance
from the shadow world of work.

Last year, visiting the Bernice Garden,
I saw how you looked at
each flower individually,
studied each piece of outdoor sculpture.
When you thought no one was watching,
you slipped a folded bill
to the man who sat quietly
on a bench next to his cart
and called him Sir.

The List

Christal Ann Rice Cooper

In the Summer of 1994, something happened which led to my father and me having discussions during our nightly walks. During these discussions, we learned things that neither of us was aware of. This only deepened the pain, but it also set us free to some degree, and it made our father-daughter bond stronger.

The most conflicting and painful thing for me were some of the fears I had toward my dad that I had no reason to have. It was so crushing to my conscience. I was responsible for these fears. It would be so easy to blame it on the wolves. But when it came between my dad and I was responsible and he was the victim.

It was my goal to make it up to him. Then to realize it was my goal to make it up to myself for depriving myself from having a deeper father-daughter relationship. So instead of focusing on the fears, unhappiness, the terror and the darkness, I focus on the things he did that only fathers who love their children do.

So below is my list of all the healthy, uplifting, and loving things my dad did for me:

1. I was a bed wetter and my father never made me feel ashamed and never punished me for that.

2. In Germany, we had a slumber party and I had a sleepwalking nightmare. I found myself in bed and I knew that my dad had carried me.
3. My father dressed up as a monster for Halloween and hid in the bushes to say "boo!" as my sister and me came home from school.
4. My dad taught me how to hold an armadillo and took a photo of me holding it.
5. My father told me that my first-grade teacher in Del Rio, Texas felt that I should repeat first grade. He said that it was my choice but that if I chose to repeat first grade, I would live one year longer.
6. My dad picked up my mother, my sister, and me from the Frankfurt, Germany airport and he gave my sister and I chocolate and racecars.
7. My father took my sister and me to the toy store on Spangdahlem Air Force Base in Germany. I found a "Charlie's Angels" game that I loved but I didn't have enough money. My father noticed that there was some kind of imperfection to the game and he showed the manager. She lowered the price so I had enough money to get the game.
8. My dad taught my sister and me how to wrestle. We had a huge black mat in the attic of our house in Germany. At the time, I didn't like it at all. But I realized that he was trying to teach us to be strong and to defend ourselves.
9. My father would come home from work and take my sister and me out front of our house in Germany and we all three played catch with the baseball and baseball gloves he gave to us.

10. My dad mended our scrapes that every child gets in life by administering alcohol and peroxide. When we would cry, he would say something to make us feel better.
11. On Christmas Eve, my father told me to look out my bedroom window into the sky and that I would be able to see Santa Clause and his sleigh. I looked out but couldn't see them and I got upset. He told me if you look out real close and real hard you should be able to see Santa and his sleigh. I looked out and I saw Santa and his sleigh. I was excited.
12. Dad always made us think. And yet at the same time he taught us to have imaginations and that magic was a right that all children should experience. It was Christmas and my dad asked my sister and I how Santa Clause could possibly deliver all these presents to all the children in the world in one night.
13. My father taught my sister and me how to make a drum. He ordered a cow skin, made a mixture, and put the mixture and cow skin in a huge barrel. My sister and I in our bikinis had to continue to stomp on the cow skin in the barrel. He then punched holes in the cow skin and tied it with cords placed within a humongous wooden frame. He placed it on the balcony of our German home to let it dry in the sun. He got a huge wine barrel and hired a local artist to draw an Indian image on the skin. I have that drum to this day in my Indian guest bedroom in my home.
14. Every place we lived, my dad would always have a swing for me. As a little girl and even a teenager, I

would spend hours swinging so I always felt he did that just for me.
15. All the times my father took me to the library.
16. My dad trusted me to take his old-fashioned video camera and film to school for a project.
17. My father taught me how to hook a worm and fish.
18. My dad taught me how to gut a fish.
19. One night in Germany, I kept on seeing Hitler's face. It made me afraid, and I'd cry. My father let me sleep in their room on the floor. He even showed me it wasn't really Hitler, because when he'd turn on the light the image of Hitler would disappear.
20. My dad loved to play hide and seek with my sister and me. He would hide twinkies in a certain place and we had to find them. One time we found them in the dryer.
21. My father allowed me to read whatever I wanted, and this mattered so much because I was a voracious reader and sought reading as an escape.
22. My dad respected my privacy, knocking on my bedroom door, never going through my journals or my room.
23. My father reared us to believe and rely on the Gospel. The greatest thing he did.
24. My dad tried to teach me the Lawrence Welk dance. After a few steps I gave up. This is one of my greatest regrets.
25. My father trusted me to borrow books from his own personal library.
26. I was very white and sweated very easily; I would

break out in hives when near grass and under the sun. My dad never made me do outdoor chores during the summers or anytime it was hot.

27. My father taught me how to chop wood with his own tools. This was my favorite chore because it was cold outside, and I'd never sweat or breakout.

28. I failed French and Chemistry and other courses. I tried my best – and when I told my dad that I failed he did not get on to me. He said all that mattered is that I tried.

29. My father trusted me to take his green metal canoe out on the lake behind our house on Sylvan Drive in Kathleen, Georgia. My best friend Renee and I would take that canoe and just let if float on the lake while we read romance books.

30. My dad taught my sister and me how to box so we could defend ourselves.

31. My father taught me that any woman could do anything by telling me about Margaret Thatcher and showing me books he had on mechanics written by women.

32. One Christmas, Santa got me a Bee Gee album, but it was only an instrumental album to their music. I cried and my dad told my mom to buy me a real Bee Gee album.

33. In Germany, I didn't want to go to Brownies anymore. My father said that was fine, but I had to tell the Brownie troop leader that I wasn't coming back.

34. One time while in Bonaire, Georgia, I got sick. The

doctor said I was not to eat anything for twenty-four hours. My mother made fried chicken and I cried and begged for a piece of chicken. My dad gave me a piece of chicken.
35. Our parents dropped my sister and me off at the theater to see. *In Search of the Historical Jesus*. There was that scene when Jesus pitched a fit when He overturned the tables due to the people gambling in the temple. When my father picked us up we told him about that scene and that we didn't believe it. He said that it really happened and pointed out the Bible verse when we got home.
36. I tried out for basketball in the seventh grade. My dad would come by after work and sit in the bleachers and take me home after practice. I didn't make the team, only to realize that I did it to make him proud. But he never shamed me or made me feel bad about not making the team.
37. My father taught us how to play Cat, Dog, or Horse with the basketball.
38. Even though I hated it, my dad had me (with his help) work on my car—putting in an engine and a transmission. He did it to make me strong.
39. My father attended Southside Baptist Church, the church I went to, with me. It was on Pleasent Hill Dr. in Warner Robins, Georgia. I know he wanted to join the church, but wouldn't so I could belong to the church on my own.
40. I inherited my love for the Dallas Cowboys from my dad. My dad would allow me to stay home from

church when Dallas was the first team to play, that way I wouldn't miss any of the game.

41. One time in the Sylvan Drive house, I had a bad nightmare where I fell off the bed with a big thud. My father came in to make sure I was okay.

42. When we first moved to Georgia from Germany, I shoplifted a tube of lipstick. My dad had me go to the manager and the manager talked to me about how wrong it was.

43. My father taught my sister and I how to Indian dance and we danced in one of the Pow Wows wearing Indian outfits my mother made for us.

44. My dad told me things about his life that were true. Also there were revelations he told me about. I recorded all the stories into my journals, so I'd never forget and as something to leave for my sons.

45. My father taught me how to ride my bicycle when we were in Texas.

46. My dad told me about the new series "American Justice" with Bill Kurtis that came out. And I've been watching that series ever since.

47. When my father had chores to do outside while a Dallas Cowboy game was on, he never made me do chores. My only job was to tell him how the Dallas Cowboys were doing.

48. One time I was so angry with my dad. I was chopping wood on our landlord's land, and my dad was a distance away. I cried and called him every name, which I am ashamed to say. I know he heard me but he never got on to me for that.

49. My father taught me the different games of checkers. He would openly cheat without my realizing it, and then before I could go he would tell me to look at the board very carefully, showing me what he had done. He was teaching me to be observant.
50. My dad taught me how to play poker, though we'd never bet money.
51. My father would play Old Maid with my sister and me.
52. My dad told me about his lifelong dream of owning a ranch in Alaska.
53. I learned my love of fiction from my mom, but my love for nonfiction and poetry came from my father. One book in particular I still love is *Lame Deer, Seeker of Visions: The Life of a Sioux Medicine Man*. I did a report on it for English. Eventually I ended up buying my own copy.
54. My dad was driving me to work at Robins Federal Credit Union. On the way there, we noticed two women and a wheelchair in a yard. One woman was standing and the other was on the grass. It was obvious that the woman fell out of the chair and the other woman was not strong enough to put her back in the chair. My dad said we should stop to help her put her back in the chair, and we did.
55. When my sister and I were little, my father would make us homemade ice cream.
56. One time when I was two years old, my dad, on his way home from work, encountered a huge bull frog. He stopped to pick it up and showed it to me and my

sister in the bathroom.

57. One time I wanted to go for a long walk, but my mother and sister did not want to. My brother was just a baby. So my father walked with me and we started counting how many big worms we passed during our walk.

58. My dad and my toddler brother had a surprise for my sister and me. When we got into the entry way of our home, we were greeted by two wild hens.

59. Anytime my father came across a newspaper article he thought I'd be interested in, he would let me know about it.

60. Every Sunday, my dad, my sister, and I would play the picture game from the paper. They had two cartoon pictures and you had to figure out the ten differences between the pictures.

61. I was net fishing across the street from our house where there was a pond. They were emptying the pond and allowed the neighborhood kids to get a net, walk in the pond, and catch something. I fell and a chuck of flesh from my knee the size of a quarter was sliced off. My mom took me to the emergency room and my father came by to make sure I was okay.

62. My dad gave me two pieces of advice: make sure that you invest something from the money you earn, and make sure that whatever you decide to do for a living is something you are passionate about, because most of your life will be working.

63. My father would always be the one to read instructions, put our toys together, and show us the directions on how to play with them.

64. One time I was afraid of a movie that had blood, but my dad told me it was only ketchup, and I wasn't afraid anymore.
65. My father always told me he loved my long hair, which made me feel good since my mother's and sister's hair was short.
66. My dad would give me and my sister rides on the hood of his car. We never got hurt and we thought it was fun.
67. My father trusted me to drive his truck.
68. When we were little, my dad would allow my sister and me to play with his hair and put barrettes on his hair.
69. While in Germany, my father and my mom gave huge parties with food and soda or tea. Never alcohol. We all created a big circle and sang the "Hokey Pokey" song.
70. My dad never drank and always taught us that every alcoholic was once a moderation drinker.
71. My father would sometimes smoke cigars and a pipe. He used to put the cigars in a box in the refrigerator. He quit due to my brother having breathing issues.
72. My dad would always get phone calls from a man named Billy who had special needs. He always took the time to talk to Billy.
73. One time my father donated his vacation leave for a co-worker who desperately needed to be off work but didn't have enough time accumulated.
74. My dad took my mother, my sister, and me to visit his high school teacher. The high school teacher gave my sister and me each a dime.

75. One time I wanted to watch *Ode to Billy Joe* and my father wanted to watch *The Old Man and The Sea*. He let me watch *Ode to Billy Joe* and we only owned one television.
76. One time I told my dad I smelled smoke, only to have him tell me I had a stuffed-up nose, and he gave me medicine to make me feel better.
77. I was so hot in my room. My father gave me advice—something he learned working with his dad in the oil fields. Soak your sheet with cold water and then sleep beneath the wet sheet with a fan blowing. When you wake up you are cool and dry in the morning. And it worked.
78. My dad also gave me other advice: when you get a new pair of shoes, put them on and then soak them in water. The shoes will be able to be worn without any pain or marks.
79. My father passed on his relationship with animals to his children: we made friends with deer, bunnies, snakes, wildcats, racoons, fish, horses, turtles, frogs, dogs, alligators, and chickens.
80. My dad took the time to take me hunting, though I did not enjoy it. All I could do was talk and dad told me. I was scaring the squirrels away.
81. My father let me borrow Slade—his black gun—to take for my shooting class with the Warner Robins Police Department.
82. My dad told me about a man who got into a woman's unlocked car while she was at a stop light. He said that I should always make sure I lock my car door

first. Now the first thing I do when I get into my car is lock it. Then I start the car and put on my seat belt.
83. My father let me put on as much makeup as I wanted.
84. My dad always made sure we had shelter and food on the table. And any money he received, he would give to my mother for her to disperse as she saw fit.
85. I have funny memories, like when I was getting my military ID card. The man asked my father my birth date and my father looked at me. He couldn't remember.
86. Dad taught me the best way to eat chocolate chip cookies: in a bowl of milk, soaking—yum.
87. My father knew how much I loved Mary Tyler Moore and read an article about her new comedy (that didn't do well). He came up to my room, knocked, and talked to me about Mary Tyler Moore even though he wasn't interested. He was just interested in what I was interested in.
88. In 1981, *On Golden Pond* came out and I was desperate to see it. My dad dropped my sister and brother off at one theater and I cried when they were not playing it at that theater. He drove to the other theater so I could see it.
89. My father is the perfect example of what it means to forgive.
90. No matter what, my dad loves his three children—I am the middle child. My sister is two years older than me, my brother is eight years younger than me.

I shared part of this list—but only the top ten—to my father for Father's Day a few years ago, and he was deeply touched. I plan on sharing this with my dad once I reach

100.

It is true that there are always good things one can say about their father, and it appears that he is a good father based on those things he has done.

But I think what makes a good father is not only doing these things but having the right motive behind every good deed or even the right motive behind what his children perceive to be negative.

And I am my father's child.

And I am so proud to be his daughter.

Team Hoyt

Pete Black

"*If you are unwilling to risk the unusual, you will have to settle for the ordinary.*"

—Jim Rohn

1977, Holland, Massachusetts: Dick Hoyt was exhausted, and he had two more miles to go. His legs and back ached, and his heart pounded. In his entire life, he had never run more than a mile. Yet at age thirty-seven, he was running in a five-mile race. His fifteen-year old son, Rick, had convinced him to participate in a benefit run for a high school lacrosse player who had been paralyzed in an accident.

Dick's challenge was made more difficult because he was pushing Rick in a wheelchair. They finished the race next to last, but when they finally crossed the finish line, Rick said to his father, "Dad, when I'm running, it feels like I'm not handicapped." On that day, Team Hoyt was formed, and a life-transforming journey was begun.

During Rick Hoyt's birth in January 1962, the umbilical cord was wrapped around his neck resulting in oxygen deprivation to his brain. The official diagnosis was spastic quadriplegia with cerebral palsy. When Rick was nine months old, doctors suggested to the Hoyts that they institutionalize him, concluding their assessment with the awful words, "He'll never be more than a vegetable."

The Hoyts ignored the doctors' advice. They were convinced their baby had a level of intelligence because his eyes followed them around the room. They found hope at Children's Hospital in Boston, where they met a doctor who encouraged them to treat Rick like any other child. Judy Hoyt spent countless hours teaching Rick the alphabet. At age eleven, he was fitted with a computer, and by pecking out words on a keyboard, he was able to communicate verbally for the first time.

Rick's first words were "Go Boston Bruins." The computer enabled Rick to go to public schools, and he graduated from Boston College in 1993 with a degree in special education. Later he worked at Boston College, helping develop communication systems for people with disabilities.

After running that first race in 1977, Dick became obsessed with competing with Rick and did so as often as possible. Dick and Rick Hoyt have competed in races around the world. In 1992, they biked and ran 3,735 miles across the U.S. in just forty-five days. Team Hoyt finished the Hawaii Ironman Triathlon, one of the most grueling athletic competitions on the planet, six times. In the Ironman, Dick swam 2.2 miles while pulling Rick in a small raft connected by a bungee to Dick's vest. Upon exiting the water, Dick placed Rick's 100 pounds on a specially equipped bicycle and rode 112 miles. And following the bike portion, Dick lifted Rick into his wheelchair and ran the final 26.2-mile marathon to the finish line. Their best finish time in Hawaii was thirteen hours and forty-three minutes.

Team Hoyt completed the Boston Marathon, their favorite race, thirty-eight times. April 8, 2013 was to be Dick's last Boston, and a bronze statue honoring the Hoyts was dedicated before the race. However, they were unable to complete the marathon. They were three miles from the finish line when terrorists exploded two bombs near the finish line. Because they were stopped by officials, and unable to complete the race, they returned in 2014 to honor their commitment.

Now forty-two years and more than 1,100 races later, Dick, age seventy-nine, and Rick, fifty-one, still compete, although Dick has retired from marathon distances. A friend pushes Rick in the longer races. Team Hoyt's list of events includes 70 marathons, 94 half-marathons, 216 ten-kilometer runs, and 247 triathlons. Rick was once asked if he could give his father one thing, what would it be?" He responded on his computer, "The thing I'd most like is for my dad to sit in the wheelchair and I would push him to the finish line. No question about it, my dad is the father of the century."

Highway 11

Judy Benowitz

Valerie drives her ten-year-old Camry onto the dirt road which cuts across the open pasture of her forty-acre farm. A dust cloud kicks up behind her as she winds past a hundred- year-old cattle loading dock. A crisp, warm day in Georgia, but Valerie doesn't notice. She parks next to her house, a small, one-room cabin with a wrap-around covered porch. Two fishing ponds out front are separated by a grassy walkway. A hammock hangs between two large sweet gum trees.

Valerie's steps are heavy as she enters the house with her small packages. As it is almost Christmas, she has bought books for her grandchildren. She carefully wraps each one, leaving them on the kitchen counter along with a receipt that reads 4:08 p.m. In the bathroom, she opens the medicine cabinet and takes four Xanax. Outside she finds the garden hose and duct tape in the shed. She comes back for a paper and pencil as almost an afterthought. In a wooded area on her property, she parks in a small clearing and gets out to attach the garden hose to the tail pipe.

My husband Bob and I had just returned home from visiting Valerie's family when the rabbi called. He wanted our son Brett to address the congregation about being a college freshman. I was stunned that the rabbi called me on the most terrible day. "You are an angel sent to me today. My sister committed suicide."

The phone suddenly went dead. I thought maybe he wasn't prepared to counsel me, and I hung up. He called back ten minutes later and told me his brother committed suicide years ago. We talked for a long time, and he helped me get through that day.

After Valerie died, I looked back to our childhood for a clue that would indicate that she had a suicidal personality. I thought maybe I had contributed to it by lording over her like a big sister, sucking all her power and energy, and using it to advance myself. Maybe one day I would be suicidal. Could it be a defective gene that shows itself later in life? Two of our cousins also took their lives. Does it run in the family? Is it depression? Could I have saved her?

"Don't beat yourself up. You are not a trained clinician. You could not know what to do," my friend, the marriage and family counselor, had said.

This is what suicide does to a family. The questions never stop. "It's the gift that keeps on giving," the rabbi said when I told him why we could not come to the temple that night.

When Valerie died, I went back to school to learn how to write a book. I had always kept a journal, and I had published a short story about my mother. Valerie ended her life, but I knew I could never do that. Life upon life were not enough for me. How were we so different? I wanted to tell her story, but the story became about me.

Valerie lived in that little town of Monroe all her life, while I moved away as soon as I bought a car, always looking for the next adventure. And it all started on Highway 11, that swath of road between Monroe and Winder, Georgia, where we grew up. It was a whiskey-soaked, Southern Baptist upbringing in a blue-collar family.

1953-1963

I was so small I could barely see out the back window of that old car. There wasn't much to see anyway—just an empty landscape with trees in the distance. But there was a road beneath me. Through the rusted-out floorboard, I could see each stone in the asphalt when the car stopped. The road blurred with dizzying speed when the car started moving again. I wanted to know where that road would lead.

"Follow the beer cans to Winder," Uncle Perry Hugh said.

Monroe was in a dry county, but Winder had plenty of beer joints. He and my dad frequented those beer joints or bought moonshine from the local bootleggers.

Dad drove to a house deep in the woods for moonshine. Down a dirt road, the house sat in a clearing. It stood on rock pilings. Dogs lounged about in the yard.

"Stay in the car." Dad slammed the door.

We three kids, ages eight, six, and four, sat in the back seat of that 1939 Buick Roadmaster convertible. Peering out the window, we watched our father walk up the wooden steps to the bare porch.

He disappeared inside the darkness of the open door to

make the transaction. After a few minutes, little black faces peeked out. They looked to be our age.

One by one, they stood in the doorway, stuck out their tongue, and disappeared back inside. A barefoot boy came first, maybe eight years old, wearing white shorts and no shirt. Next came a girl with braids framing her face. She wore a white dress made from a flour sack. We could tell it was once a flour sack because we could see part of the upside down "Pride of Sussex" logo. A younger boy wearing a white shirt and shorts stepped into the doorway, and the little girl came last, a two-year-old, also in a flour sack dress. Like the others, she stuck out her tongue then went back inside.

The kids reappeared, standing side by side in a row across the porch—a parade of pink tongues against black faces. We laughed as our father walked down the steps with his purchase.

We called him Dan because Mother did, even though all the church ladies said we would go to hell for calling our father by his first name.

"Never mind those busybodies," Mother said. "You'll have to do something much worse than that to go to hell." Mother had a way of taking the fear out of life.

While she practiced the strict Southern Baptist rules by taking us kids to church and Vacation Bible School, Dan sat on the couch watching Billy Graham on TV. When the local preacher stopped by to invite Dan to church, he hid in the bedroom until the reverend drove off. To him, church was women's work.

Dan drank white lightnin' from a Mason jar. I tasted it once, after I saw him gulp it from a paper sack in the kitchen.

Well, I didn't really taste it because as soon as I brought the jar to my lips the fumes made my eyes and nostrils burn. The Indians were right. It was fire water. I understood why it knocked him into a snore on the couch. He spent many weekends that way, and Mother complained constantly that they never did anything because he was drunk. He wasn't a mean drunk. In fact, he was sweet.

Still, my mother advised me, "Never marry a drinking man," and I didn't.

On Monday mornings after drunken weekends, Dan was up at dawn to go to work for the Rural Electric Association, the "REA," in his red truck. A lineman for the county, the kind of man Glen Campbell sang about, he wore blue work clothes. I remember waking one night to see Dan dressed in his rain gear, and mother's anxious expression, as a storm thundered outside.

"Where're you going, Dan?" I asked.

"He's going on a trouble call. Someone has lost their 'lectricity," Mother said.

Dan looked large and powerful dressed for the storm to save the world from electrical outages.

The REA was part of President Roosevelt's "New Deal" in 1933 designed to supply electricity to poor rural communities. Dan worked there as a young man and easily transitioned to running telegraph poles throughout South Africa during World War II. He was stationed in Johannesburg, or as he called it "J-burg," and talked often about his experiences there, until we told him, "We've heard that story a million times."

When he came home from the war, he never wanted to leave again.

Dan married my mother after she asked, "How 'bout it?"

Mother once told me Dan was falling-down drunk when she met him. I asked her why she wanted him. She said she loved him. I guess she thought she could fix him. Women do that. They pick a fixer-upper to marry and then complain when he won't fix. I learned that many years later from Doctor Laura, a radio talk-show host. People called in, complaining about their love life. Her first question was, "Were they like that when you met them?" Invariably the answer was, "Yes." Then Doctor Laura in all her wisdom would ask, "What did you expect?"

They were sweethearts before Mother joined the Navy WAVES based in Washington, DC. She, along with twenty-seven thousand other women, supported the war effort. I learned after she died that Dan never wrote to her while he was away. Afraid he wouldn't come back, he wanted her to find someone else. Who knows? Maybe he really hoped Mother would marry another man, so she wouldn't nag him the rest of his life.

***

Dan was a storyteller. He described his first swimsuit as cut-off overalls that dragged him to the bottom of the pond he tried to cross. He rode ol' Bess the mule when she took off without him. "Ears laid back, nostrils flared, and I'm hanging onto her mane for dear life, running next to her. 'Boogety, Boogety, Boogety.'" Dan made the face of a mule and used his arms to describe her flight.

His best stories were about drinking. One of my favorites was when he and Uncle Perry Hugh picked up some moonshine one Saturday afternoon. My brother Wayne and our cousin Jimmy sat in the back seat with the liquor. When the car broke down on the side of the road, Perry Hugh and Dan got out and walked to the neighbor's house to make a phone call, leaving the two boys in the car. The police had stopped to offer their assistance, when Wayne hung out the back window holding a paper sack and shouted, "Hey, Dan, you forgot your liquor."

These memories aren't mine, but stories repeated often to boisterous laughter at family gatherings. But I do have a clear childhood memory of sitting outside on a paint-chipped bench rocker with my dad on a hot summer night before we had air-conditioning. It was the coolest place to be in the South. Under the dark, star-lit sky he sang "Carolina Moon" in his booming baritone voice—first, way down low, and then way up high. I can still hear it. He smelled of hooch and Camel cigarettes, a salty blend I will always remember.

Years after that night, when I was a teenager, I asked him, "What are you living for?" His answer was simple: "To provide for you kids."

There were three of us.

Wayne was two years older than me—small and bespectacled with thick lenses that magnified his eyes. He had worn them for as long as I could remember. At one church Easter egg hunt, he took them off because they bothered him. Later, they were found in the road, smashed by a car. He wore his glasses all the time after that.

He had two best friends: Jimmy Whitley, who was big and strong, and Jimmy Harris, our cousin who once wrestled Wayne to the ground and pinned him in a contest to see who was tougher. Mother watched the struggle from the window before coming outside to pull cousin

Jimmy off her boy.

"I had him," Wayne said, frustrated. "Go back inside."

Wayne's friend Jimmy Whitley had a crush on our younger sister Valerie and carried her around like a little trophy when she was small. I chased after them because I wanted to be carried, too, but no way. He only wanted Valerie.

She was a beautiful child with blond hair and green eyes. Her lovely skin got tan in the summer while Wayne and I, with our red hair and freckles, sunburned easily.

These flashbulb images come back to me as a collage of life in that white-framed house, where there was no running water, but there was electricity.

A single light bulb hung from the ceiling to brighten the small, sparsely furnished living room. In the winter, my father built a fire every morning to warm our house. He crouched, holding a sheet of newspaper over the opening of the fireplace. It sucked against the iron grate, producing a vacuum so all the smoke would draw up the chimney and not into the house. When he pulled the paper away, the fire was brilliant. I thought Dan had magic.

Mother made breakfast in the next room on an iron, wood-burning stove that provided a little heat in the kitchen. In the corner stood a wringer washer. I remember the time Mother's hand got stuck between those two large cylinders. She let out a scream and somehow released their grasp. They popped open to free her hand.

We played outside in our big front yard that was dirt, except for the large roots sprouting from a giant oak tree. Mother swept up the twigs and acorns with a brush broom that left a pattern of strokes. The yard looked neat and clean after a fresh brooming.

A piece of cotton stuck in the hole of the screen door kept out the flies. A large stone replaced one of the broken steps. Many pictures of us kids were snapped there, like a scene from *The Grapes of Wrath*.

Our dog Thunder had puppies every season until Mother said, "That's enough. You need to shoot that dog."

Dan took his rifle and shot Thunder between her eyes. I watched him out the window. Then he threw up and buried the dog. That was animal control in those days. He never shot another thing until many years later when I was in high school. Then he shot a giant rat that took refuge in one of our shrubs. I watched as he blew it right out of the bush. It was gross.

The outhouse, a small wooden structure with one hole, was off the back porch, a short distance along a little path. The first time I sat on it, I thought I would fall in. Leaning over my knees, I inched my little hiney over the hole to keep my balance. A Sears and Roebuck catalog was on the floor in case we needed paper. The thin sheets did the job, but I was glad when eventually we got toilet paper.

As the homestead slowly modernized, a coal-burning stove stood in the fireplace. Wayne leaned against it one morning, warming himself in his new winter jacket before school. A metal shape from the stove branded the back of the jacket. Furious, Mother made him wear it anyway because we couldn't afford another one. He wore it every day to school, pretending he didn't care because it was in the back, and he couldn't see it. A tough kid, he rode to school in my dad's truck and was gone all day. I couldn't wait to go to school and get out of that boring house. Mother made me take naps, along with Valerie, who would soon become my little charge.

One cold Christmas morning, Wayne and I ran outside to see the brightly colored swing set from Santa. We walked that swing set across the yard, swinging high, almost turning it over, before our dad sunk the legs into the ground with concrete for our safety. That's when Mother put Valerie on the teeter-totter with me and instructed me to go slow.

At two years old, she couldn't hold on and fell to the ground. I realized then that if she was going to play with me and couldn't keep up, she was going to be a total pain.

She was my little shadow for years. I remember complaining to Dan that Valerie was always following me around and getting in my way.

"That's because you are her big sister. She looks up to you and wants to be like you," he said.

She followed me into a black iron pot that stood in the front yard, a remnant of bygone days when it was used for heating water over a fire pit, maybe for washing clothes. It looked like a cauldron a witch might stand over as she stirred up a potion. When it filled with rainwater, Valerie and I climbed in for a bath. After we splashed about for a while, we stepped out blacker than the pot. Ordinarily we bathed in a number two galvanized steal washtub in water drawn from the well and heated on the stove.

"Valerie, I want to use your towel," I said after a bath one day.

Unyielding, she stood on it. I tried coaxing, bribing, and

trickery to get her off, but she wouldn't budge, so I pulled it out from under her. She fell and bumped her head. It was easy to push her around, if I had to.

That night at dinner—or another night like that night—Valerie, swinging a butcher knife, chased me around the kitchen table.

"Mother, help me!" I cried.

She ignored us and continued washing dishes, as if she was deaf. I ran, ducking and shielding myself with my hands, incredulous that Mother didn't care. Valerie cut me on the little finger before Mother dried her hands and took the knife away. I can't remember what I did to deserve the attack.

After having three children in seven years, I understand why Mother would take her time breaking up a fight. If she ran every time one of us called her, she would never get her housework done.

One afternoon, seemly like so many others, I heard Mother calling from far away. I ran from the woods behind our house. "What is it?"

"Where have you three been?" she demanded.

"We went to the woods."

"Well, who said you could go?" Her face looked like a wasp's. "You're getting a whipping!"

"What about Wayne and Valerie? They went, too."

"Yeah, but whose idea was it?"

I wasn't sure, but Mother seemed to know.

***

On summer nights, Mother and Dan sat on the front porch drinking beer with salt poured around the top of the can. Imitating them, we poured salt in our Coke cans and watched it foam. My dad smoked cigarettes and flipped the butts into the front yard where we played. Stepping on them with our bare feet, we got burned, but no one cared. It was a hazard of being Dan's kid.

To the left of the house stood a well, where Dan drew our daily water supply. We stood clear of the iron crank, as the metal bucket attached to a rope dropped into the dark hole. The log that held the rope in place as it wound was slowed by hand and smooth from so many turns. The taste of that cold water from a metal dipper was sweet.

In those olden days, arsenic was used in mice traps. Our parents laughed as they told the story of how they thought Wayne and I once poured arsenic into the well. We were too young to remember. Maybe we didn't and simply left the box on the side of the well after plundering the kitchen. Not sure that's what we did, Dan took a long time bailing out the well, just to be safe.

The well was covered by a small wooden roof with a bench underneath where my cousin Jimmy and I—at ages six and five—played doctor. I laid on my stomach, and Jimmy tugged down my shorts, exposing my bottom. He put his ear on my backside to listen. I could feel his crew-cut hair, warm and fuzzy.

"Judy, you need to come inside. Jimmy, it's time for you to go home," Mother shouted from the kitchen window.

"Yes ma'am," Jimmy said and jumped on his bike. He lived just up the road, a few doors down.

I pulled up my pants and came inside. "Why does he have to go?" I asked.

"It's time for him to go home, and you need to keep your pants up."

There wasn't much to do in rural Georgia in the fifties but watch the grass grow or listen to a prop plane's distant sound in the sky and wonder where it was going.

Underneath a peach tree with its low hanging branches, Mother swept a floor for our playhouse. With concrete blocks she made seats for us, and she stacked small planks with Pet Milk cans and invented a cupboard. Our imaginations ran wild under that fragrant foliage.

Valerie and I played pretend with our cousins Ann and Wanda.

"Okay, pretend we live in a castle."

"I'm the youngest and the prettiest."

"You're the mean big sister."

"I have to hide from you."

"You be the prince, and you have to kiss me."

"You're the mother, and you try to rescue me."

We made up elaborate stories and scripts, and they all hinged on being the youngest and the prettiest.

"Okay, let's play."

"I'm the youngest and the prettiest," I shouted.

Whoever shouted that first, of course, had the best part.

Years later as I recall these scripts we fleshed out, I see that I was jealous of my pretty little sister.

I had a nightmare that haunted me for many years. I dreamed in color, that Valerie and I were playing catch at our grandmother's house when a bull broke into the yard and chased us. We ran around the house a few times with the bull hot on our heels, snorting. I made it to the front door and ran inside to safety, but Valerie didn't come in. As I closed the door, I saw the bull gore her to death. He walked away leaving her lifeless body on the ground, a tragic forecast.

***

Our grandmother lived across Highway 11 from our cousins. We called her Mama because that was Mother's name for her. One afternoon we stopped to visit Mama when our cousins came down their driveway and stood on one side of Highway 11. We stood on the other side.

"Stay right here," Dan told us.

Dressed in their Sunday best, everyone else stood there waiting when I made a run for it to be the first one across the road.

"Judy, stop!" Dan shouted.

Tires screeched as the car bearing down on me stopped just in time. Everyone had been waiting for it to pass before crossing.

"No one told me," I said.

"Yeah, you heard me, but you weren't listening," Dan retorted.

My family jokingly referred to me as "Delayed Reaction." I was slow on the pick-up of conversation, and my responses were late because I wasn't paying attention.

I wasn't the smartest kid. When I peeked at my permanent record in fourth grade, alongside the string of C's, Mrs. Breedlove had written "poor child" next to my name. Shocked and embarrassed, I had no idea I was poor till then. My dad made six thousand dollars a year. Most of my friends were from blue-collar families like us.

When I was in third grade, we had built a new house on the four acres across the street from our old house. We had one car parked in the carport and one bathroom in the three-bedroom brick house where Valerie and I shared a room. Mother made many of the clothes Valerie and I wore, except for socks and underwear, which we got for Christmas. That's what poverty looked like back then.

Wayne and Valerie had the top grades in their class and earned a trip to the Ice Capades in Atlanta. I didn't go because my scores weren't high enough. I felt like a real loser compared to my siblings. Dan teased me, too, which didn't help.

Valerie competed with me at everything. We wore the same clothes, had many of the same friends, and even looked alike in high school.

No one encouraged me to go to college except my tenth-grade English teacher, who wanted me to switch to a college prep curriculum. To catch up, I took courses, including plane geometry, with my sister who was two years younger. It was a challenge to outscore Valerie. Sometimes I think she deliberately threw a test just to keep peace at home. Our competition grew to range wars. We fought about everything: clothes, friends, academics, tennis rackets, and whose turn it was to do the dishes.

My relationship with my brother wasn't as testy. We got along most of the time. While he was a compassionate little guy, Wayne could be mean to his sister. He once called me out of class in grade school. As I walked slowly to the door to see him, he shouted "Come 'ere, goot!" which was slang for goat. Everyone laughed, and I was embarrassed.

Another night, I tiptoed behind Wayne to scare him when he swung around and socked me in the face. I don't think he meant to. He wanted to scare me right back, but I was following too close. Years later he would warn me not to follow him and Whit to the woods by tagging me in the back with a BB gun to make sure I understood. Dan seemed unconcerned since it didn't break the skin.

Wayne wasn't much of a hunter. He got a rifle for Christmas one year and headed to the woods to shoot something. Through the kitchen door, I watched him walk across the garden with his gun. When a rabbit ran out and startled him, he jumped back on one foot, pulled his rifle up, and shot it in an instant. He was happy for his success but sad for the rabbit. I don't think he shot anything but tin cans after that, except when he shot me in the back with that BB gun.

And he wasn't the best fighter, either. In fifth grade he got into a scuffle with a bigger kid who jumped on him and broke his leg. He wore a cast up to his hip for a long time. It had a rubber heel to help him walk. He could go at a good pace, swinging that leg around him like Chester on *Gunsmoke*. Years later he had lower back pain and did a series of exercises for it. I suspect the pain resulted from the cast with the rubber heel not being even with his other leg.

That summer after fifth grade, while playing baseball, he ran back to catch a fly ball and tripped on the edge of the road, knocking himself out. When I came into his room to see him, he was in bed, and all his friends were standing around talking and laughing. I quickly left.

"Why don't you go in there?" Dan asked.

"There're too many boys."

"You know all of them." He studied me.

"They'll laugh at me."

I did not want to see Gawyn, who stood at Wayne's bedside smiling at me. Gawyn was my age and once had asked me, "Are you an Indian? You have a red face, and your hair is red. You look like an Indian."

In fact, I am part Indian. Dan described his grandmother as a full-blooded Cherokee squaw. Like many southern families, we have Indians in our heritage.

Gawyn was the reason I left the room that day as my face reddened with embarrassment, but in high school he would be my first prom date.

***

Wayne started drinking as soon as he started driving, and his misadventures continued. On many nights Dan got a phone call from the local police to "Come pick up your boy" because Wayne was drunk. Every time the phone rang late at night Mother and Dan dreaded learning who was on the other end. It was always the police about Wayne.

When he came back from Vietnam, he was shell-shocked and paranoid and didn't want to be around large crowds or strangers. His personality changed, and he wasn't comfortable around his family either. It took a long time for him to adjust to civilian life.

He went to work for the Rural Electric Association, like our dad, and he got married. He survived those teenage years and the Vietnam War, but he was the first death in the family. Somehow, we knew he would be.

In 1985, while living in California, I came home for a rare visit. Dan and I browsed through some old black-and-white photos. Wayne, at age five, not wearing his glasses, was sitting up in bed with a fresh flat-top haircut.

"Look how cross-eyed he is," I laughed.

"Don't make fun of Wayne," Dan said. "Don't ever make fun of Wayne."

He had died ten years earlier.

***

My dad had a third-grade education. He dropped out of school at age ten to help run the farm with his mother and his younger siblings after his father died from a measles epidemic in 1922. His mother home schooled him. During the depression, the family lost the farm. He was a father figure to his siblings. He grew up fast and always felt a responsibility for his family, and maybe moonshine was his method of coping.

Mine was a whiskey-soaked upbringing, probably the reason I enjoy my martini cocktail hour today. Riding in that Buick Roadmaster Convertible may have inspired the purchase of my first car, the 1968 MGB convertible. When my dad sat on that couch, watching Billy Graham on TV, I came to believe there was more than one way to find God. I converted to Judaism when I married Bob.

Dan entertained us with his storytelling, and his story deserves to be told. He passed away in 1989 before my sister took her life. I am glad he was not there to know her end.

Dad

Daniel Michael

We learned about duty from history lessons of great men like George Washington, Teddy Roosevelt, Robert E. Lee, and others. Each one had to make hard choices and followed the course of duty each time to resolve their problems, whether they were personal or national challenges, it didn't matter.

Even with those epic men and their incredible contributions, discovering what duty really means has been best displayed to me by my dad.

In a day when duty is often scoffed at and freedom is sought after more than responsibility, I was reminded of what liberty really is: Liberty is the duty and opportunity to do the right thing. I am always at liberty to do right, but never at liberty to shirk my duty.

I thought that was a good definition, as my dad exemplified it all through his life. When I think about what he went through growing up, I am reminded about some of the stories that were shared with me over time. Heroes always look larger the further time progresses, but these are just samplings of the life of one man, who exemplifies duty at its fundamental definition.

The morning was cool, but not as cold as it had been that early spring. It was also early morning, very early. No light was visible as he stood on the edge of the porch facing north in the direction of the barn. Edgar was watching for that telltale sign that his dad had the mules hitched and was ready to start plowing. How would he know? He watched for the momentary glow from the tip of his dad's hand-rolled cigarette, for that was the sign his dad was waiting for "first light" to take the mules to the field and start the day's work.

This was a six-day-a-week routine, mind you. Not something he did on the weekends. Not a hobby farm that produced a handful of eggs each week. No, it was a matter of life and death. If crops failed, the family went hungry. There was no welfare program or food stamps for hungry farmers in the Tennessee Valley of North Alabama.

Once the mules were hitched, his dad would take time for his one, and often only, smoke of the day while waiting for enough light to be able to head to the field for the day's work. Edgar would follow the intermittent glow of the cigarette to the barn and sit and wait with his dad for the first light.

"Dad, what would you talk about while you sat there waiting for the sunrise?" I asked. "No son," he answered, "you don't understand, we were not waiting for sunrise, we were waiting for first light, just enough light to plow a straight row. Sunrise always came later!"

With no electricity, no flashlights, Edgar learned to work when there was light, and sleep when it was dark. It was just the way of life on the small farm in Lexington, Alabama. I asked Dad how they lit their house, and he said it was with kerosene lanterns, and the cleanest globes you could imagine, because any dirt or smudges on the globes would dim the already meager light coming from the single flame. Hollywood makes kerosene lanterns seem romantic and nostalgic in a way that was hardly accurate. Sitting at the kitchen table working on a homework assignment meant having the lantern dead center of the table while all the children sat with their books pushed as close to the lantern as possible to make out the writing.

At night, as the family prepared for bed, he said his dad would be sitting in front of the fireplace with a piece of cedar, slowly cutting little slender pieces of wood to have in the morning to restart the fire. He said he could still smell that cedar odor and see the perfectly sharpened pocketknife that was his dad's constant companion. When asked one day if he had his knife with him, his dad responded, "I have my pants on, don't I?"

Dad said he didn't know they were poor. He thought most people lived like them. If a car passed on the dirt road, they would step outside to watch it whiz by at breakneck speeds of sometimes twenty or twenty-five miles per hour! Once, a truck ran over one of their chickens, and to avoid a substantial loss, his mother yelled, "Go grab that chicken before it cools down and I will pluck it for supper!"

For years, a pistol and shotgun hung over the door of their wood frame home, and though the guns hung within reach of every child in the house, no one touched them, because his dad taught them that they were tools, not toys, and their duty was to use them properly, not play with them. And tools they were! Dad was squirrel hunting by the time he was six years old. He was allowed to take a single shot .22 caliber rifle to the woods, by himself, and often would return with several trophy squirrels and a rabbit if he was really lucky.

Much of this was transferred into my own dad's mentality about life in general. Life was full of tools that were not toys, and these tools for life were to be used properly, not wasted by idle play time. Nothing, he said, was ever built by playing with toys.

While my dad heartily agreed with this principle, he never restricted toys from his children, but at the same time, our toys could not interfere with our duties at home. I distinctly remember coming home from school one day and I couldn't find my bicycle. I was sure it was stolen. But alas, after searching in vain, my mother informed me it was left lying in the yard the night before, and when my father got home from his midnight shift early that morning, he confiscated it and locked it up. Until I could learn my duty, I couldn't play with my bike. Wow! I was devastated. But as you might guess, I never, ever again left my bike laying in the yard when the day ended!

It was some time around his eleventh or twelfth birthday that Edgar's dad, Mac, took a job with the very secretive installation in Tennessee known as Oak Ridge. He hired on as a carpenter to build barracks. The only problem was that he was leaving a family behind, a wife and several children. Edgar, being the oldest boy, would be tasked with "running" the farm. That consisted of managing a cotton field, corn field, a kitchen garden, which was not small, several farm animals and nearly a dozen beehives. Falling behind in his studies, he had to repeat a grade that year because he simply couldn't be in two places at once. Either his school studies would suffer, or the farm would fail; it was not a difficult choice, because by age twelve, Edgar had already developed the character of a grown man. One grew up fast when his family depended upon him.

Those teenage years were not the rebellious years of a young man trying to find his way, no; rather, it was a teen boy doing the work of a man and feeling the strains on the body and mind of carrying a load not designed for someone of such a small frame. He became lean and strong in those years, and picking a fight with him might leave one with hurt feelings and a bloody nose.

He recalls with fondness learning what the life of a farmer that had literally a few irons in the fire was like. His dad owned a blacksmith shop. It was right there on the farm, and when he was not working in the field, he was busy repairing wagon springs, wagon wheels and hitches, and farm implements. He also made a fair living shoeing horses as well. Most of these trades were passed on to Edgar, though he didn't have much opportunity to use them in later life, but the character developed from performing his duties as his dad's helper was exercised over and over and on a daily basis.

Before he was ever a teenager, the local phone company came through to run phone lines to the big city of Lexington. He had a strong mule and was hired for a dollar a day to pull the lines. He worked the same hours that the men on the job worked, completing the job and then handing the money over to his dad for the support of the farm. This was, in his mind, his duty. He would be hired out at times to help other farmers as they didn't have sons to help them, and always at the end, he offered the money to his own dad, who had to do without his help during those days he was away from his own farm. It was his duty.

He learned duty and hard work by watching his mother come in from the woods with a basket filled with various herbs and nuts and berries that would end up on the table that evening as part of a meager supper. He realized that a bountiful meal was when they were all together, not just when their bellies were full.

He recalls defending his home from a crazed billy goat that got loose and turned over his mother's wash pot and proceeded to tear down their screen door going into their kitchen! He said the goat stood nearly as tall as him, but he and his dad corralled the goat and removed him from the property.

While it seems humorous, one must remember that washing laundry meant hauling water from a deep seventy-foot well with a two-gallon bucket, filling the wash pot, keeping the fire hot, and stirring the clothes, then wringing them out and hanging them till dry. All of this had to be repeated that day because of the crazed critter!

Edgar left the farm at eighteen and headed to Pearl Harbor, arriving at a base that was still picking up the pieces from the attack by Japan only a few years earlier. He served his time in the military, coming home only once on leave to bury his dad.

It was at this time that a decision had to be made: Stay in the military and finish his commitment or return home to care for his mother and the farm. Because he had sisters and a brother who had learned many of the same excellent character traits from their mother and dad, he could safely leave his home in their care until he completed his duty. Again, it was all about duty.

He married when he was out of the military, and he drove busses, managed a gas station of which he was part owner, did mechanic work and sheet metal aviation work, and even sold insurance for a short time. All the while, his duty to his family never slacked. I asked him once how much he was making on his job when he got married, and he said $1.30 an hour, but he got a pretty good raise within ninety days of that, and was making almost $1.70! He was rolling in the money!

All of that said, he was able to buy his first house the year before I was born, paying a whopping $16,000 for a three-bedroom, one-bath house on about an acre and a half of land. It was on that tiny piece of property that Dad took dominion of the earth seriously. Dominion, in the simplest definition, is bringing order out of chaos. By wrestling undergrowth, uneven ground and rocky soil, he turned that little, tiny piece of property into something much more.

He planted a half-acre of corn every year, and he maintained a flock of chickens, a small herd of goats, and often ducks, and always Tennessee Walker horses. He trained them to compete in horse shows. These regal creatures would be taught by my dad to step in that famous Tennessee Walker style, which garnered him several trophies, as both me and my sister rode competitively for several years.

I remember once when my dad hooked the horses to

a plow and was turning the garden, which was a little over a half-acre, and someone saw him and complained that he shouldn't be using such fine horses that were bred to be show horses! Dad smiled and explained that if the "pretty horses" couldn't be used for something more practical than "showing off" he didn't need them. He even expected his horses to do their duty!

He labored all of my growing up years for an aluminum recycling plant, starting as hired labor and finally advancing to foreman; he chose retirement shortly after I joined the military. When I asked him why he would have retired at fifty-five years old, he told me of how his dad died. His dad was also an employee at the same aluminum recycling plant years earlier, when Dad was just eighteen years old. At fifty-five years old, his dad was tasked with getting a gasoline pump started that had problems with the motor. He said his dad tugged and pulled on the starting cord and dropped dead of a heart attack that day. Dad said, "I turned fifty-five, and standing there in that same plant, I took stock of my life and made a decision, that I had too much to do and probably not enough years to get it all done, and I was not going to miss the opportunity to accomplish more." So with that decision, he took an early retirement, and has now been retired more years than he actually worked for the company.

As I said though, he didn't retire to sit on his laurels, but rather got busy building custom furniture, remodeling his home, getting more involved in his local church and finally traveling the country with Mom. He didn't slow down but actually said he might need to get a job in order to get some rest!

Gritty Southern Fatherhood – 135

Traveling from one end of the country to the other, they hit every small and large town they could, sometimes being gone for upwards of six months at a time. It was during one of those long stints away from home that I had some struggles and was having some challenges of my own. He heard about it and hooked up the camper, hopped in his truck, and headed straight back home to help us through a particularly difficult time. His duty toward his family trumped any fun or recreation he was having in his retirement.

I remember him telling me as I was leaving from Nashville to join the military that I should keep my head low and do my duty. He said, "Don't go out there to be a hero, go out there to do the job you are assigned. Do it the best you can, and that will be reward enough."

Duty. It seems that has always been his watchword. Family helping family was ingrained into me by stories of barn raising, and other community-based stories that usually surrounded helping someone afloat while someone was sick, or through the loss of a structure by fire or storm.

An uncle of my dad's didn't care for a particular family in town, and while he was gone working out of town as many men in that region had to do to keep their farms afloat, his house burned. His family was safe, but all was lost. Dad said the very family that his uncle cared little for, along with a group of Amish folks, went into the woods and cut the timber and rebuilt his house in just a few days. They would not take any compensation at all for their work, and all the while they camped outside and cooked around a campfire for the entire process.

We moved Mom and Dad onto our property back a

few years ago, and are thankful for that decision, as health problems have plagued both of them since that time. Now at ninety-three, a cancer survivor and still making sure farm animals are cared for daily, a garden is put in each season, and the yard is kept pristine, he still does his duty. Mom has suffered three strokes and is legally blind, and Dad cooks their breakfast each day, cleans up her crumbs as she has trouble knowing if there is food on her fork or not, keeps the bathrooms clean, and makes sure the floors are mopped once a week. That's in addition to working in his shop and keeping things repaired around the farm.

We have told him, "These are your golden years, so why don't you sit down and relax?" His response? "I want to leave this place for you better than when I got here, I don't have time to sit down; simply too much to do!" So, we don't get in his way (very often) and let him have run of the property. It works out nicely for me, as I have a full-time job and couldn't begin to dedicate the time it would take to keep our hobby farm up and running at this level.

Just this morning, I went over before sunrise for our routine cup of coffee and sat in the living room with him and chatted about things he wanted to get done today. His shoulder hurts today a little more than it did yesterday, and he didn't sleep as well as he would have liked, but he was still making plans for the day...he is still doing his duty.

The Fishing Trip That Never Happened

Bill King

When I was younger, I didn't understand why Dad was hardly ever home. As I grew older, I came to realize the reason was that he worked all the time. It would be years before I understood why he worked so hard and for such long hours. In fact, that understanding would not come until after he was long gone, and I was a grown man.

More than anything else, I wanted time with him. What time I did spend with him meant me joining him at work, rather than him doing the things I wanted him to do with me. He had no hobbies, at least none that he actually did. He wasn't being selfish, because he rarely did anything for himself. I believed he loved me, even though he never actually told me so. I wasn't so sure that he liked me, because of the small amount of time he spent with me. Because I never actually had much opportunity to sit down with him and ask the questions I needed answered, it has taken me most of my life to figure some of them out. Others I may never know.

As a child, my dad knew the toughest of times. He

experienced them firsthand. He grew up during perhaps the hardest economic decade in American history. He turned thirteen years old the same year the stock market crashed and The Great Depression began. Being a teenager during that time was as far removed from being a teenager now as the East is from the West. Many teenagers now have everything they need and most of what they want. From what Dad told me, he and his family barely had the necessities of life, let alone the luxuries. About the only thing that kept them from starving to death was the fact that they lived on a farm. That meant they raised their own vegetables, had chickens for eggs, had a cow for milk and butter, and raised other animals for meat. About the only things they bought at the store were flour, sugar, and coffee. Sometimes they didn't even buy sugar. Instead, they sweetened their food with syrup they had made from the cane they raised. All the things we might think about when we consider life as a teenager were certainly not the things he experienced.

I remember hearing my dad say that he grew up so poor that he couldn't rub two nickels together. I didn't realize for a long time that he couldn't do that because he didn't have two nickels. That may have been a slight exaggeration on his part, but probably not much of one. His father was a poor Southern sharecropper in West Georgia. By the time my dad became a teenager, his education was long over. In fact, his last year to attend school had been several years before then. By the end of the third grade, he had learned to read, write, and do arithmetic. Perhaps he believed that would equip him well enough to work on the farm. Maybe his father (my grandfather), thought so too, because he allowed him to drop out. For whatever reason, Dad never returned to school. He became a full-time farmer after that year. I'm not sure exactly how old he was when he dropped out, but he was close to six feet tall and still in the third grade. That was not because he was dumb, but because every fall he had to stay out of school to pick cotton and work the farm. By the time he got back to school, he was too far behind to catch up.

They called a field that had not previously been cleared and farmed "new ground." That new ground was often full of stumps, roots, and rocks, not to mention hard, red Georgia clay. Plowing new ground behind a mule was a tough and hot, sweaty task. To add insult to injury, Dad often plowed that new ground with no shoes on his feet. He wore shoes in cold weather, but once summer came, off came the shoes. The injury on one occasion was caused by a stinging scorpion that he stepped on. Dad never forgot those days and how difficult life was back then. One thing was for certain, he never wanted to have to live that way again, and he didn't want that life for his children either.

I was his fourth and final child. He was thirty-nine years old when I was born. I think when my two older brothers were growing up, he had a little more time for them. Even then, much of that was time they spent working together on their family farm. According to my brothers, he did take the time to carry them fishing, occasionally. By the time my older sister came along, they had left the farm. Dad opened his first business, which was a small restaurant with a bowling alley in back. The bowling alley consisted of two lanes. There were no automatic pin setters back then. When someone wanted to bowl, my brothers served as the pin boys. Six months after I was born, Dad sold the restaurant and bought a house that came with three acres of land. He opened a new business on the front parcel of that land. I didn't know this back then, but I think rather than Dad running the business, his business ran him. As I look back on it, maybe he was like someone in water that was over his head. He had to swim or sink. He swam frantically, simply to keep his business afloat and to, as they say, "make ends meet." I also believe he remembered those hard days of his youth when they had nothing, and he feared going there again. I can certainly respect him for that.

In most ways, my dad was not a bad father. In fact, he was a good man who modeled several behaviors that I have tried my best to emulate in my own life. He was perhaps the most honest person I've ever known. He owned a business where he sold many things by weight. Whether it was coal, sand, or gravel, every ton he sold always weighed 2,000 pounds. If anything, they might have weighed a little over, but never under. I remember once when he had gone to the bank and they gave him back too much money. It was only one dollar, and the bank was in a neighboring town, fifteen miles away. Rather than keeping the money, or waiting until the next time he went to the bank, he turned right around and drove back there to give back that dollar.

I can't remember a single time when he lied to me. If he ever did, I didn't know it. He was a Christian who never drank alcohol or did drugs, and who rarely ever cursed. Periodically, he let a four-letter word or two slip out, but I never once heard him take God's name in vain. He smoked fat Swisher Sweet cigars, occasionally. He was a strong disciplinarian, but he never abused us. He was over six feet tall and weighed close to 300 pounds. When I was younger, I thought he was the biggest man in the world, as well as the strongest. I remember thinking that his hands were so big that they looked like hams on the ends of his arms. He was such a large man that usually all he had to do was tell me to do something. I was too afraid to not do what he said. Morally and ethically, I could not have asked for a better father. He did, however, have a major flaw as a father, in my opinion. I vowed if I ever had children of my own, that I would not do what he had done.

Although I never heard him say so, I don't think Dad ever had much opportunity to be a child. Being a child in those days was obviously much different from being a child these days. I think for my father, his childhood may have even been a little harder than most. Instead of playing, he spent his time working the farm. Since he dropped out of school at such a young age, he was never a member of any school-sponsored sports teams. Life was tough and time was precious. Instead of playing games, he spent his time working the farm. I'm not sure that he ever even attended a football or baseball game, either as a child or as an adult. I guess because of that, he never had much interest in sports as an adult. I loved to watch sports on television. Football was my favorite, but I watched them all. I even watched hockey, which was unusual since I lived in the South. We had no hockey teams down here back then. As much as I might have wanted him to, Dad had no interest in sitting down with me and watching a game. He didn't know anything about them. He probably didn't know a quarterback from a goalie! Once when I was watching hockey he asked, "Boy, what are you watching?" When I answered, "Hockey," he said, "Is that what they are knocking around on the floor with those sticks?" I don't mean to whine, but I never remember one single time when we tossed around the football, or when we played catch with a baseball.

During his lifetime Dad did three things. He farmed, owned and operated a couple of businesses, and drove a semi-truck. He never made much money, or if he did his expenses consumed most of it. He saw to it that we always had a roof over our heads, clothes on our backs, shoes on our feet, and plenty to eat, but that meant we rarely saw him. He worked long hours and days and did so every day except Sundays. Often, he had already left for work when I got up each morning, and he didn't get home until I had already gone to bed, or was about to do so.

I loved my dad, and although I can't remember him ever telling me so, I believe he loved me. Sometimes, I wasn't so sure that he liked me. I've often heard others say that love is spelled T-I-M-E. That was the one thing my dad didn't seem to have. That one major flaw that I mentioned earlier was that he never seemed to have time to spend with me. I didn't realize it back then, but my dad was a workaholic. For the first thirteen years of my life, Dad owned and operated that second business of his. He sold heating coal and building supplies. He had his own trucks, which he and his employees used to haul what he sold from the coal mines or other suppliers. They also used his smaller trucks to make deliveries to customers. Most of the time I spent with him was spent at his business. As soon as I was old enough to handle a shovel or lift a cement block, I helped in Dad's place of business. I didn't do it for the pay. There wasn't any, except as Dad said; the clothes on my back, the food I ate, and the roof over my head. Most of the time I didn't really mind the work itself, but that wasn't the reason I did it either. One reason I did it was because Dad expected me to work, and there would have been consequences if I had not. Honestly, I think the main reason I worked there was because I wanted Dad to be pleased with me, but more importantly, that was the one place where I could spend a good bit of time with him. I especially loved to ride in the big trucks with him. The smell of burning diesel fuel still takes me back to those days. A special treat was going with him to all those exciting places to pick up the goods he sold. Those places included coal mines, coke plants, sand pits, brick and block yards, and lumber yards. My favorite of those was when I actually was allowed to go down inside the shaft of a coal mine.

Then, even that time with Dad at his work came to a sudden end. Dad closed his business and after that I saw him even less. For the next two years, he leased his trucks out to a trucking company. He drove one of them himself. He spent the last two years of his life on the road doing long-haul trucking. He was only home every week or two. Often, he even had to work on Sundays.

Now granted, I would rather have had a workaholic for a father than an alcoholic or a drug addict, but they all leave scars on their children.

One of my favorite pastimes as a child was fishing. Obviously, Dad had enjoyed fishing at one time. He had two rods and reels stashed away in the corner of his bedroom. As I mentioned earlier, I heard stories about him and my two older brothers fishing together. Unfortunately, that never happened with me.

Honestly, I can't remember what kinds of reels he had, but one of them was a brown, closed-cover reel on a fiberglass rod. The other one was an open-faced reel on an old bamboo rod. I like the closed-face one better, because I couldn't cast the other one without ending up with a bird's nest of fishing line tangled in the reel. He also had a small metal tackle box. It was brown and filled with artificial lures like a jitterbug and a sputterbug. There were the normal things in there like hooks, sinkers, floaters, and plastic worms.

Since a small fishpond was located practically in our front yard, I didn't have to travel far to go fishing. We also had a small creek that ran across our property, and a larger lake on our next-door neighbor's property. Dad and I could have easily walked a short distance to "wet a hook" together. As close as we ever came to doing that was when he showed me how to press and hold the button on his closed-face reel, and then release it as I cast.

Occasionally, he even promised he would come home early and we would go; but deep inside, I doubted that would happen. My doubts always proved to be correct. On more than one occasion, I had everything ready to go as soon as he came home. By the time he arrived, it was too dark. He did tell me that I was welcome to use his equipment any time I wanted to go. I did that quite often, but what I really wanted was for him to go with me.

There were a couple of regulars who fished in the pond

in front of our house. I often joined them. They bragged on what a great job I did casting. Their words gave me a sense of pride and made me feel special. At the same time, I longed for those words to have come from my own father. I longed for him to be the one casting beside me.

In the summer of my fifteenth year, Dad told me he was going to Florida and going deep-sea fishing. I was so excited, until he told me I couldn't go with him. He explained that he had been invited by a group of other men, and that no children were going. At fifteen, I did not see myself as a child. Long before that age, I could drive any truck or piece of equipment that he had in his business. By that time, he had already closed his business, and my oldest brother had opened an auto paint-and-body shop in Dad's building. I was learning the trade. I had already learned to spray paint. I thought of myself as a young man, but obviously Dad did not, or at least he did not think his friends would.

I suppose he saw the disappointment and hurt on my face. He said, "I'll tell you what. Next year, after winter and when the weather warms up, we'll go. Just you and me. I'll know where to go and what to do after this trip, and we will go deep-sea fishing together." That promise got him off the hook and out of the doghouse with me. I grabbed a calendar and counted the months until spring. I began planning and dreaming. I had never even seen the ocean, or the Gulf of Mexico, as it would be. I had never been on a boat any larger than a small ski boat or fishing boat. The largest body of water I had ever fished in was the Tennessee River, near my hometown in Northeast Alabama. My buddy Chuck and his family had money. That meant they had a place on the river and a boat in the boathouse. Over the next couple of summers, I spent a lot of time there with them. That summer in particular, every time we went fishing on the river, I pretended I was fishing in the Gulf of Mexico. When I reeled in a big crappie, or freshwater bass, I pretended it was a red snapper, or better yet a giant marlin!

Christmas was coming. That meant spring was the next season. I was still excited about going deep-sea fishing, so much so, that I wasn't even giving much thought to Christmas. Dad had been gone on a long-haul trip for almost two weeks. He had dropped off a load somewhere in New Mexico, picked up another load of something there, and was headed to California. I don't remember what city.

While he was still on the West Coast, he began to get sick. He had developed a cough and had a sore throat. Rather than finding a doctor out there, he brushed it off as a simple cold, and decided to head back home. He said if he didn't feel better by the time he reached home, he would go to a doctor. He had a driving partner who shared time taking the wheel on those long trips. Dad believed with his help he would be able to make it home with no problem.

By the time he reached home on that Thursday night, he was so sick and so weak he could barely get out of his truck and walk in the house. That night I sat on his bed beside him. In a voice so weak I could barely understand him, he told me he wasn't going back out on the road. Christmas was only two weeks away, so I thought he meant until after Christmas. He said, "No, I'm not ever going back out." I didn't know for sure what he meant by that, or what he planned to do, but I thought at least we might have a little more time together.

The next morning, one of my brothers drove Dad to see his doctor. The doctor diagnosed him with a severe case of strep, but his biggest concern was that Dad's sugar level was over 500. He sent him straight to the hospital to be admitted. Since the hospital was in another town that was an hour away, I stayed home. My school was not out for Christmas break yet, so I went to school that Friday. After school, I went home with my friend David and spent the night at his house. About 2:00 the next morning, I heard the telephone ringing. David's mother came into our room and told me my sister was on the phone. I already knew why before she ever said a word. On a bitterly cold December day, with snow falling, we buried my father. That may have been the day the fifteen-year-old boy became a man.

Obviously, our deep-sea fishing trip would never happen. To this day, some fifty-two years after my father's death, I still have never been saltwater fishing. As a matter of fact, I still have never fished in any body of water larger than a river or lake. More importantly than that fishing trip that never happened, I have longed simply to spend one more day with my dad. I long to talk to him as one grown man to another. Of course, that never happened, and it never will… at least not in this life.

What has happened is that I had a child of my own. Her name is Ashley. I never forgot that vow that I made all those years ago. Ashley and I had a daddy-daughter date every Thursday for most of her life until she was grown. Guess what we did on many of those dates. You got it! We went fishing! I guess I turned her into a tomboy. By the time she learned to read and write, she had also learned to bait her own hook, catch her own fish, and take it off the hook. She even chased down a big tomcat once that tried to steal a catfish she had caught. We also went to breakfast on Thursday mornings, and sometimes went for ice cream either before we went fishing or after we cleaned our catch.

Ashley is grown now and has a family of her own. She has one son. He is thirteen years old now, and his name is Drew. Drew is coming to spend the night with his Gigi and me on Friday. He and I will make a biscuit run on Saturday morning, right before we drive out to Uncle Paul's fishpond. Drew has had his own rod and reel for several years now. It's a Zebco, on a graphite rod. We will probably catch a few bream, and maybe even a bass or two, but quite honestly we really don't care if we catch anything or not. We just like to spend time together. A few years from now, we won't remember if we caught anything or not, but we will never forget that we went fishing…numerous times. Who knows, we might even go fishing in the Gulf of Mexico one of these days. Maybe his mom will go with us too.

Super Dad

Pete Black

"Impossible is just a big word thrown around by small men who find it easier to live in the world they've been given than to explore the power they have to change it. Impossible is not a fact. It's an opinion. It's a dare."

—Muhammad Ali

March 20, 1998 – Walnut Creek, California: John and Aileen Crowley were on top of the world. Thirty-year-old John had graduated from Georgetown University then received a Juris Doctor degree from Notre Dame Law School before earning an MBA from Harvard Business School. He was earning a nice salary with a top financial consulting firm in San Francisco. The young couple had two beautiful children, Megan, age fifteen months and Patrick, a week-old newborn. Then the doctor called.

John and Aileen had consulted a physician to determine why Megan wasn't walking. After receiving the test results the doctor phoned the couple with the bad news. "I am sorry," he began, "Megan has a rare genetic disorder called Pompe Disease. Most children die from respiratory failure or cardiac arrest by age two.

"There is no cure. You should enjoy the time that you have with her." Then tests revealed that Patrick also had the disease. When Megan almost died from pneumonia, John promised her he would find a special medicine to cure her.

In July 1998, John quit his job and moved the family to Princeton, New Jersey, where he joined Bristol-Myers Squibb, a large pharmaceutical company that was researching cures for diseases like Pompe. As the new marketing director in the research division, he could learn more about genetic disorders.

A year later, John learned about Novazyme, a small four-person company in Oklahoma City, Oklahoma, that focused exclusively on Pompe research. He convinced a venture capital group to invest $8 million in the company and then quit his job with Bristol-Myers and joined Novazyme. He would not let the research fail; his children's lives depended on it.

By 2001, Novazyme had yet to come up with a cure, but John, now company CEO in Boston, had quickly grown the company and sold it for $225 million to Genzyme, another biotech enterprise with the stipulation that he would join Genzyme as Senior VP and head up their Pompe research.

By this time, Megan and Patrick were both wheelchair-bound and dependent on ventilators to breathe. Both had hearts twice the normal size. Time was running out. Doctors predicted the children could not live much beyond age five, and Megan would be five in a month. John's urgency increased and he drove the research team relentlessly as they evaluated four enzymes that might provide a cure.

On a Friday night in October 2002, John got the call that Megan and Patrick had been accepted to a clinical trial involving twelve children using one of the Genzyme drugs. In early January, John and Aileen pushed the button to start the children's enzyme drip at St. Peter's University Hospital in New Brunswick, New Jersey. The children received the drug every other week.

After the first test in April, both children's hearts had reduced to normal size and their neck and shoulder muscles had grown marginally stronger. Genzyme invested $200 million in Megan and Patrick's special medicine, Myozyme. The drug has helped hundreds of children with Pompe survive.

In February 2018, John, Aileen, twenty-year-old Megan, and nineteen-year-old Patrick were recognized in the balcony of Congress by President Donald Trump at the State of the Union address as he lobbied the Food and Drug Administration to spend more money on research for genetic diseases.

Today, still in her wheelchair and supported by a round-the-clock nurse, Megan is a straight 'A' senior at Notre Dame. Patrick, also in a wheelchair, continues to live at home. Two decades after he quit his job to discover Megan's special medicine, John is the CEO of Amicus Therapeutics, a biotech company. He saved his children's lives. Now his mission is to cure them.

Hindsight

Tom McDonald

After graduating high school in 1964, my higher education options were extremely limited by financial considerations. A very small four-year college was about the only choice most graduates from the small rural high schools in the area had at that time. The primary focus of the college was to train teachers or those going into the business world. As a matter of fact, the words "Teacher's College" were in the school's name.

It was rightfully determined years ago that teachers must have a thorough background in psychology. A constant flow of psychology classes of some kind in both undergraduate and graduate school were in abundance on my schedule. Since psychology is not an exact science, there were a lot of theories bouncing around, and they continue to this very day. It was surprising to me that in every one of these courses it seemed to be an accepted fact that sons and fathers normally do not get along. Some think that as a boy begins to reach a certain age, generally in his teens, he automatically develops a rivalry with his father, sort of like they are in a territorial dispute with each other. At this point the theories begin. Maybe the father is disappointed in his own life and tries to re-live his life through his son. That would indeed cause a lot of tension. Maybe the dad creates an environment of fear and instability. Frequently, the father may not treat the son with respect as an individual in his own right and the son is resentful. Some fathers find it difficult to compromise and tend to criticize the behavior and performance of the son. The criticism could take many forms, such as academics, athletics, music, choice of friends, etc. Some sons are the exact opposite of their father, which could cause some ill will on the part of the father. Regardless of what one might believe, psychology is chock full of theories but relatively short on absolute facts.

Whatever my experience might have been in my personal life, during my years as a high school counselor it was very common for me to meet with parents and students where this conflict was in full bloom. Somewhere along the way, I read a quote attributed to Mother Teresa. It was framed and hung on the wall of my office for many years.

You will teach them to fly, but they will not fly your flight.
You will teach them to dream, but they will not dream your dream.
You will teach them to live, but they will not live your life.
Nevertheless, in every flight, in every dream, in every life the print of the way you taught them will remain.

Mother Teresa may not have had much training in the field of psychology, but she seemed to know a lot about human nature.

A theory is a theory for one reason: it could be right, or it might be wrong. Ironically, my relationship with my father was the exact opposite of what was taught in most textbooks on that sensitive topic. There is no doubt in my mind that my father did not know Mother Teresa, but he raised his children as if he did. He did not expect any of us to fly his flight, dream his dreams, or live his life.

Rejection and fear had no part in my relationship with my father. He was never abusive in any sense of the word. Today there may be a lot of confusion between what is abuse and what is discipline. Dad may have believed strongly in corporal punishment, but he was definitely not abusive. One did not have to spend much time with my dad to discover that he did not tolerate foolish behavior or disrespect in any shape or form. We were polite with adults and did not generally speak unless spoken to. I felt loved and supported by my dad. We worked together and he generally invited me along when he ran errands or did various woodworking jobs in the community. The fact that we did not share any hobbies did not seem to be a problem. His only hobby was work and mine was not.

The one absolute memory about my father was that he did not give an inch to adversity. When the wolf was howling at the door, it was met face to face with an iron will that was unbending. Dad was short of stature but was physically strong from years of manual labor. He tried to impart to his children the will to face problems head-on. He would sit and study a problem for hours until he figured out some way to accomplish what needed to be accomplished. God gave us a brain for a reason, was his policy.

My feelings about my father evolved over the years. As a child, he was my protector and a very stern disciplinarian. There was no doubt in my young mind that he would protect me with his own life if necessary. As a teenager, suddenly he became old and out of touch with what was going on in my world. But while I was still in high school, my mother passed away and we seemed to grow closer as a result. All my siblings were married and just the two of us lived in the house. The chores he assigned daily often interfered with plans conjured up with my buddies. Sports, fishing and camping on the river, and speculating about members of the opposite sex were much more important to me. However, all of this was secondary to completing whatever chores he assigned.

After I became a husband and father, his role changed once more and he became a source of advice and wise counsel about life in general. The older I got, the smarter he became. It was an amazing transformation on his part. His experience as a skilled carpenter and otherwise jack-of-all-trades proved invaluable as me and my wife undertook to build and maintain our own home. My job as a teacher didn't pay enough to buy a house or hire someone to do it for us. Dad had never shied away undertaking major tasks, and that trait was apparently inherited. Under his tutelage, we built our first home bit by bit.

Now that my wife and I are retired and our children are independent and living far away, my admiration for what my father was able to do on a very meager salary has increased dramatically. He was somehow able to raise seven children while supporting his own father and my mother's sister, both living with us for many years. Dad was the son of an iterant carpenter and was raised mostly by relatives after his mother died when he was only three years old. He quit school in the sixth grade and followed his father to various jobs across the South all the while learning to be a carpenter in his own right. He lived with his dad in a railroad boxcar with other itinerant workers in Sweetwater, Texas, for a while before coming back to Alabama. In 1918, when the Spanish flu epidemic killed millions worldwide, he took his first full-time job at a local lumber company building wooden coffins for flu victims.

His tenacity influenced me in ways I don't even realize. He married our mother in the 1920s and had three young sons when the wolf was at his door again. At the end of that decade, the Great Depression cost him his job, along with millions of other Americans, and subsequently his home. A relative allowed him to erect two tents on the back of his property, where he lived with my mother, three of my brothers, and my grandfather for three years. One tent was used for cooking. A sheet separated the kitchen area from a small cot for his father while the other tent was living quarters for my mother, father, and older brothers. A small spring was their only source of water. A daily supply was brought by bucket to the tents. The nearby woods served as their bathroom. My oldest brother was his chief assistant and together they foraged the woods for firewood they could load into a wheelbarrow and sell in the community, going door to door. The phrase "A man does what he has to do" was heard a thousand times while growing up in his house. Instead of whining and complaining about a problem, his mantra was "fix it yourself."

Daddy was determined to provide his children with a stable home and roots which he never experienced as a child. Roots and wings are the two best things a home can provide for children, and my parents were determined to accomplish both. The Great Depression put the whole world in a bind and my family suffered mightily from financial hardship. Dad told me many times to always try and prepare for what he called "hard times." He taught his children that we would experience difficult times in our life. He was convinced they never disappear permanently. Waking up every morning and not knowing if his family would be able to have enough to eat was a nightmare.

If my daddy had a bucket list while I was growing up, it was to move out into the country where he believed he would have a better opportunity to support his family. A self-sufficient person does not have to depend on others for his well-being. He purchased some property near Collinwood, Tennessee, and built a log cabin in hopes of moving his family. No passable roads, no water except a small spring at the bottom of a steep hill, and no indoor plumbing combined to make that move a no-brainer for my mother. After spending several weekends in the isolated cabin, she refused to go back. Dad finally sold the property to a relative.

As a boy, we took many Saturday pilgrimages to the country searching for a small piece of property he might afford. Some weekends it was a family trip and other times it was just the two of us. The trips were always fun for me because I shared his dream of country living. Fun does not equate to success, because we made dozens of trips over the years with absolutely no luck. He found many places he would have liked to buy but they were all out of his price range. Several years of futile searching left me wondering if we would ever live in the country, but Dad refused to give up his dream.

Finally, in 1958 he located eight acres in the west end of Lauderdale County on a narrow country lane. By splitting it with my sister and her husband, he made a deal which he could afford. At the time, the tract of land was planted with corn and there was not a tree in sight. Today, my wife and I live less than a mile from the old home place, and the trees which were planted as saplings around the yard are huge and there is shade galore. The single lane dirt road is now widened and paved. The old place is virtually unrecognizable.

My dad had an astonishing amount of confidence in his ability to accomplish virtually any task which required skill or manual labor. By virtue of osmosis or DNA, his sons followed in his footsteps to varying degrees. None of us were actual volunteers for the jobs we were assigned, but Daddy made it rather clear he was not running a debate club. We didn't have the luxury of drifting off to a mountaintop or to the gentle streets of San Francisco to try and figure out who we were or to find ourselves. If we had any doubt as to who we were, he was quick to tell us.

Daddy did not tolerate slackers. During my years working in the public schools, it was not unusual to hear children of various ages openly defy their parents and talk back to them. At times, the parents even thought it was funny when their child used profanity in their presence and refused to comply with orders to do their schoolwork and stop misbehaving in school. This was quite astonishing to me. There is no question in my mind that not a single one of W. E. McDonald's children would ever be foolish enough to talk back or refuse to do something we were told to do. He did not raise any angels, but neither did he raise any fools. He was our father and not necessarily our buddy. Not only did he serve as a judge and jury, but he was also the executioner. Due process rights were never a big topic of discussion at our house. Today's 'woke' world would be very difficult for him to handle.

Eventually, as my older brothers left for the military or started their own family, the role as his chief helper was delegated to me. Dad provided on-the-job training as a brick mason, plumber, roofer, electrician, sheet-rock hanger and finisher, painter, and, of course, carpenter. When he began to see the end of the tunnel on the construction part of our house, he staked out a spot in the back yard and told me this was where he wanted me to dig the septic tank. A word of explanation might be needed at this juncture. In rural areas without sewer lines, the waste from the house is carried by gravity into a septic tank which ideally breaks down the solid material and, by way of field lines, distributes the liquid into a wide area where it dissipates into the soil. The hole into which the tank fits is roughly eight feet deep, eight feet long, and about six feet wide. This size is sufficient to hold a 500-gallon concrete tank. Dad handed me a pick and a shovel and told me to call him if I had any questions. It took a good while to complete the project, but I learned a great deal about perseverance and manual labor. In those days, it was not unusual to pass a chain gang, prisoners chained together, along the side of a road digging ditches. Adults were always quick to point out that was what we would spend our lives doing if we didn't go to school and get a good education. We heard the same thing from our teachers. Mercifully, he hired a guy with a backhoe to dig several hundred feet of trenches for the field lines. This decision was not made to show mercy toward me, but he was in a hurry to get moved in.

My older brothers had also been given tasks that involved a lot of arduous digging. When we still lived in East Florence, he decided our house needed a cellar. This was before my time, but my daddy already had a sufficient number of sons strong enough to handle a pick and shovel. Over a period of about a year, they labored underneath our house like a bunch of coal miners and, when finished, the old house had a cellar with dirt walls and a dirt floor. It would not have made suitable living quarters but was good enough for storage and a small workshop. The extra space beneath the house allowed enough room for the installation of a floor gas furnace after I was born. We had lived with a big, pot-bellied coal burning stove that barely heated the living room. The rest of the house was uncomfortably cold during the winter months. It seemed to take forever to knock the edge off the lingering cold when we got out of bed every morning. The gas furnace kept the house remarkably warm, not to mention the fact that there was no more coal to be hauled to the heater and no ashes to be taken to the back yard and dumped.

During one particularly rough stretch, when he was desperate for a job, he applied for a rumored opening at the Tennessee Valley Authority (TVA) as a sheet metal worker. It didn't matter that he had absolutely no training or skill in that trade. He did what he had to do. His reasoning was that by the time the supervisor figured out he was not a certified sheet metal worker he would be the best one they had. It worked! He was hired and spent thirty-five years working for the TVA. He retired in the mid-1960s and bought a country store. I was in college at the time and in bad need of funds. He hired me to pump gas, air up the tires, check the oil, wash the window, stock shelves, and help folks who needed it carry their groceries to the car. The job had its challenges. For some reason, automotive engineers designed some cars with the gas cap hidden from view. Early on, it was a challenge for me to figure out where to put the gas. Some caps were hidden behind the tag and some behind one of the taillights. There was very little uniformity. Some of the drivers seemed to take a great deal of delight in watching me find the gas cap. But the most amazing part of this job was he actually paid me to work for him. That was a first for both of us.

It should be quite obvious that I loved my dad dearly, respected him above what I am capable of describing, and admired him above all others I have ever known. All my life, when people found out that he was my father, many times the conversation quickly turned to what a good and respected man he was. Many folks had stories about how he had helped them out sometime during their life. One time, I encountered a fellow by the name of Holt who ran a store not far from where my family lived during the first years of the Great Depression. He said my dad came in one day and asked him if he would be willing to sell him groceries for his family on credit. He had no job but promised to repay every penny when he was able. Mr. Holt was willing to extend credit, as he did to others in the same predicament, until they were back on their feet financially. The reason he wanted me to hear his story was because my dad did repay him every cent he owed when he was able to find a job. He went on to tell me that others he had extended credit to were not so considerate.

In spite of all the inherent good my daddy displayed toward family and friends, he was not perfect by any means. Without a doubt he did his very best to teach his children how to survive in a dog-eat-dog world without taking undue advantage of others. The proof is in the pudding. All seven of his adult children turned out to be pretty decent citizens, even with the bar set reasonably high. However, the man his children felt was the best father in the world would be described as a racist by the standards of today. The thing is he didn't know it and neither did his children until much later in life. No matter how smart or capable a person might be, the truth of the matter is a person doesn't know what he doesn't know. Racism was never a part of our vocabulary.

While in college, there was a lot of discussion about factors which influence a person's behavior. Is hereditary the most important factor or is it environment? Some believe the genetic traits handed down by one's parents influence the make-up of a person. A well-known philosopher by the name of John Locke took the position that every person is born with a mind that is blank, or a clean slate. Everything that is later written on that slate is determined by life's experiences. My experience as an educator led me to side with Locke. A child learns through observation. If you are born into an aristocratic society, you learn all the finer things about how to be an aristocrat. Those born into a family of talented musicians generally follow in their footsteps. A child whose family were cattle rustlers and horse thieves might be expected to do the same. If you are born on the wrong side of the track, so to speak, your behavior will most likely reflect what you observed as you grew up.

Daddy was born into a world still reeling from the effect and aftermath of the Civil War. His world was filled with grizzled veterans of that conflict. His own grandfather was a veteran of the Confederate army. His mother died when he was only three years old, and he was raised mostly by relatives. The stories he heard as a child were not those fairy tales where everyone lived happily ever after, but those of destruction, near starvation, and mistreatment during the period known as Reconstruction. It was a dog-eat-dog world bursting with competition for every penny and morsel. A societal pecking order was established centuries before he came into the world and, in short, that was the way it was. The adults in his world did not question the status quo and neither did he.

Indeed, there were some who saw clearly the inherent wrongs of a society which elevated itself only by keeping a foot upon the neck of an entire race of people, but those voices went largely unheeded. Generally, they had no platform to speak from and their call for change was pushed aside. Too many remained silent, and the injustice continued for generation upon generation. Thankfully, the winds of change were beginning to blow, but not soon enough for a child born in 1903.

My dad taught his children many, many good and useful things. He was a wonderful father in every sense of the word. He loved his family deeply and without question. There is no doubt he denied himself many things in order to provide for his children. But one thing he failed to do was to teach us that racism was wrong. That is not to say that we were taught to discriminate against anyone. In hindsight, as difficult as it is to believe, it probably never occurred to him that it was wrong. He simply parroted the society he grew up in.

Racism was not an overt behavior on his part but was implied. To the best of my knowledge, there were no physical acts of violence involved toward any minority. His behavior toward African Americans was never one of respect, but simply displayed a distinct lack of civility. As with many adults of that time period, the N-word was used with absolutely no understanding that it was a very offensive racial slur. My generation followed the lemmings to the edge of the cliff and dove right over the edge. We showed little, or no, inclination to do things any differently from our forefathers.

Unbeknownst to my dad, an act by President John F. Kennedy in 1961 set into motion an event which caused a drastic change in my mode of thought toward people not like me. It was my sophomore year in high school when President Kennedy unveiled his idea of what came to be called the Peace Corp. The Peace Corp was his brainchild and birthed by executive order in 1961. A short time later it was approved and funded by Congress and exists to this very day.

The Peace Corp was an entirely volunteer agency. The term of service was for two years which began after a training period of about three months. Volunteers could be of any age, sex, religion, sexual orientation, or marital status. A very nominal salary sufficient to exist in the assigned area was provided. The Peace Corp was meant to be a very inclusive organization. These people generally served in deprived areas, both in the United States and abroad, where their particular skills and training would be valuable to the local populace. For example, in 1966, Lillian Carter, mother of former U S. President Jimmy Carter, served for two years in India at the age of 68.

The three-month training period for these volunteers took place all over the country, preferably near government facilities with classroom space and dining facilities. They were generally housed with locals. One such training site was at the TVA campus near my home. The facility still exists in Muscle Shoals, Alabama, and was part of the New Deal established by President Franklin D. Roosevelt to alleviate poverty in the region. My dad was employed there as a carpenter along with several hundred other white-collar and blue-collar workers. The TVA was a major employer in the region for many years. While in training, the on-site cafeteria was utilized to feed the large group of volunteers.

My dad began working for the TVA in the 1930s, after having worked to build Wilson Dam that spanned the Tennessee River. His long tenure caused him to know virtually everyone at the plant. One of his very good friends was the fellow who managed the cafeteria. Always eager to put his sons to work, Dad told me one afternoon that they would be hiring part-time workers in the cafeteria to help with the overflow caused by the Peace Corp people, and his friend was willing to put me to work. At the time, I was 16 years old and a sophomore in high school. My afternoons happened to be unencumbered. I was hired to work after school and on weekends for the duration of the training period.

Each school day my schedule was to rush home, change clothes, and drive to Muscle Shoals to begin work at 4 o'clock. It was my responsibility to wash dishes and keep all the pots and pans ready for the cooks. After feeding everyone and before closing for the night, I swept and wet-mopped the cafeteria and kitchen floor. Other duties included everything the cafeteria manager told me to do, like help unload supply trucks as they arrived on the loading dock. My schedule was the same on both Saturday and Sunday, with my workday usually ending around 10 p.m. These late-night hours during the school week stretched the child labor laws of the time, but nobody cared. The pay was good and the work, compared to working with Dad, was a piece of cake. Besides, it was a privilege for me to be a firsthand observer of what was a history-making event.

It was during the late-night hours of sweeping and mopping the floor that my young eyes began to observe a drastic difference between what was taking place all around me at my job and what growing up in the Deep South led me to believe to be true. There was a big difference. The Peace Corp volunteers were assembled from across the country which meant they did not necessarily share my background and values. They were male and female and Black and White, mostly in their early 20s. It was common practice for them to linger after they finished eating and talk very informally with each other about the events of the day.

Invariably, my boss wanted to get home as early as possible, so he usually had me begin my cleaning duties before the trainees cleared out of the cafeteria. From the business end of a broom and a mop, I was able to observe for the first time in my young life Black and White folks mingling together as equals. There was no eavesdropping on my part. They were just talking informally. Probably, from their perspective, they did not notice me. Who pays any attention to a teenage boy mopping the floor? It was obvious their interest in each other was genuine. There was no reason for them to pretend to be interested in what the others were saying. This was not a one-time observation, but occurred daily for the duration of my employment. Maybe my young age of 16 made me very impressionable. Regardless, it made a very big difference in my life from that point on because maybe, just maybe, many of the truths we thought we knew about race were wrong. Dad was right about so many things, but he was sure wrong about at least one really big thing. The winds of change became a headwind for my dad but a tailwind for me.

My experience with the Peace Corp folks did alter my outlook on how people should be treated. It absolutely changed the way my children were raised. They were taught to be courteous and respectful to everyone, regardless of color. The N-word was taboo around our house. Societal mingling with those of another color was not a taboo.

However, my own experience did not do much for the

way my dad viewed minorities. We had many discussions about that topic over the next several years, but my father was a very stubborn man. He saw no reason to change. If it ain't broke, don't fix it, was his policy. Dad lived to the ripe old age of eighty-seven and became more generous and more loving as the years passed, but he never changed his outlook toward minorities. This regret has been with me all my life.

On many occasions during my time walking this planet, my brain has pondered how on earth the situation between the races ever reached such low levels. How could anyone living amidst injustice at every turn not have the foresight to figure out what seems so shockingly obvious in hindsight? If the Jim Crow laws which forced racial segregation were not wrong, then nothing was wrong. Looking back, it should have been as plain as the nose on our face. If simple logic could not win out, conscience should have stepped in. According to the poet Robert Frost, at some point in our lives we sometimes travel a road which diverges into two separate paths. The one we choose makes all the difference in the way we live our lives. Only, hindsight is 20/20, while foresight is never that precise. Maybe, someday.

Buzzards in a Cedar Tree

Corinda Marsh

Jolene sat on the front porch every morning from 5:00 am to 7:00 am. Sometimes it was dark; sometimes it wasn't. Sometimes as many as ten trucks passed her house during that time, but she didn't even blink when they crossed her line of vision. She was focused, but nobody could figure out what she was focused on. That drove some of them nuts.

The house at 1945 Hill Road had been there for more than 100 years. Nothing had changed. Jolene was born right there in that house in the back room where the chifferobe was—and the trunk. Everybody had a trunk. They just had different stuff in them. Most of the trunks held secrets and at least one patchwork quilt.

Jolene was the only one left. All the rest were either in the cemetery across the road or lost. Dust churned up by the pickup trucks coming down the road filled all the little carved words in the tombstones and made them look like maps to somewhere else. Occasionally cars came down the road, but they didn't churn up much dust—usually.

Jolene sat like a stone. That big white streak down the middle of her hair looked like a white mane on a fancy rodeo horse. That streak had been there all her life. Now the rest of her hair was turning gray so the streak didn't stand out much. She wasn't really old enough to have gray hair, but that's the way it was in her family. All the women got white headed early, but that was better than what happened to the men—they got bald. The parts of her hair that hadn't already turned white were still black as soot, just like her daddy's hair. She always wore her hair twisted up in two buns, one on each side of her head. At least that much was balanced.

The day Jolene was born, her mama's sister, Hortense, said, "Essie Mae, that youngun is marked. That streak down her head is a streak of bad, plum bad, I tell you!" Essie Mae didn't pay no mind to her sister. Hortense always was the crazy one. Jolene's hair was just like her daddy's except for that white streak. Hortense's hair hung like a wet dishrag down the back of her head. It was about the color of an old dishrag too, but when Jolene was young, she had a head full of thick black hair that looked like satin when the sun hit it. Her hair was the only thing about her that was soft and silky, but her hair was silky, no doubt about that. She didn't wear silk either. She was a farm girl. She wore farm clothes, and she played in mud puddles, dress and all.

Hortense never did like Jolene's daddy. He wasn't their *kind*. He came from different folks. They didn't even dress like her folks. She asked him one day why he didn't braid his hair and stick a feather in it. He told her he was good-looking enough without our feathers, but he suggested she go out to the chicken coop and snatch some red feathers out of the rooster's tail and stick them in her hair. He said it would be an improvement. Jolene thought it was funny, but

Hortense didn't. She stomped off in a huff and slammed the door so hard it shook the porch railing loose.

Jolene's daddy didn't ever like Hortense, but she was family, so he put up with her. That didn't mean he was upset when she up and died on Halloween. He figured that was appropriate. Jolene was thirteen at the time, so she didn't understand why he thought it was funny.

Hortense was across the road in the graveyard three holes down from Jolene's mama and daddy. She never married, but she knew all about babies and how to raise them. She told Essie Mae everything she was doing wrong raising Jolene. She said if Essie Mae had listened to her, Jolene definitely would not have gotten into whatever trouble she was in at the moment. And Essie Mae never failed to remind Hortense that if she had listened to her, Hortense would have had her own husband and children to raise, and she definitely would not have had to live with Essie Mae, who was, by the way, forced to add on to her house so her sister would have a roof over her head. They got even. They always got even. Jolene's daddy grumbled a lot when he had to build a room for Hortense, but he did it anyway—she was family.

Jolene's house looked like a regular house. The kitchen had a sink, a stove, and one of those old iceboxes people used before they had electricity. She had a regular refrigerator, but it was sitting on the back porch next to the cracked mirror. One clean plate and one glass were sitting beside the sink on a white dishrag with frazzles on the end. Another white plate sat on the table with a fork, a knife, and a spoon on a clean, starched white napkin. A crystal glass etched with little flowers was beside the plate.

Anyway, Jolene didn't know exactly what she was looking for, but she was sure it would be coming down that road one day, and she would know it when she saw it. Everybody thought she was looking *at* something, but she was looking *for* something. Jolene's focus was intense. She'd thrust her head forward and her bottom lip poked out like she was mad at somebody. She'd wrinkle up her brow and stare like she knew something was there, but she couldn't quite see it.

One morning just before 7:00, Jolene finally saw a car coming down the road. It wasn't a truck, but an actual car—a 1957 Cadillac. It had big old fins on the back and chrome—lots of chrome—and it was a convertible, with the top down. The Caddy stopped abruptly in front of Jolene's house, throwing up a cloud of yellow dust. The woman driving the Caddy had a fancy purple scarf wrapped around her hair. She wore big tortoise-shell sunglasses. All she needed to look like a Hollywood star was a long cigarette holder.

The Caddy had pulled up right beside Jolene's fence, and when the dust settled, the woman hollered, "Miss Jolene, I presume?"

Jolene crooked her head around and replied, "Who wants to know?" Jolene sat stone still in the shade of the dilapidated porch.

The woman whipped off the scarf to reveal bleached blonde hair, the kind with a few orange spots here and there where the bleach didn't quite take. Next she removed her over-sized sunglasses with a gloved hand and replied with her snooty face, "Miss Van Arbuckle, of the Dothan Van Arbuckles."

"Well, lah-de-dah. Am I supposed to know who the *Dothan Van Arbuckles* are?" Jolene asked.

"I should certainly hope so," the woman replied, raised eyebrows and all.

"Sorry, sister. Ain't got a clue," said Jolene.

"I should have guessed. Your poor mother never told you about us, did she?"

"Maybe you've got a hearing problem. I already told you, I don't know who you are!" Jolene said, getting more irritated every minute. She stood up and glared at the woman getting out of the Caddy and walking toward the gate.

When Jolene stepped out into the bright sun, she shaded her eyes with her hand, but the visitor could clearly see the warm caramel color of Jolene's face. She first hesitated then advanced toward the gate.

Just as the woman put her gloved hand on the gate, Jolene said, "I wouldn't do that if I was you."

The woman drew her hand back and asked, "And why is that?"

"Because Barkley don't like strangers."

"And who exactly is Barkley?"

"He's a mean old ugly cur what don't like strangers."

"Oh," the woman said as she inched back toward the car.

"Miss Jolene, I've come to bring you something, and I'd very much appreciate it if you would leash your dog and allow me to enter. It is quite warm today, and I could certainly use a drink of cold water," the woman said. Her curiosity was shoving her forward in spite of her distaste for her surroundings.

Jolene cocked her head to the side and studied the woman before she replied, "Miss Whoever-You-Are, I don't feed and water strangers. There's a soda fountain in town. I'm sure they've got plenty of cold water."

"Cut the crap, Jolene. I'm sure as hell not here because I think I might *like* you! I'm here because, through some bizarre freak of nature, apparently I am your sister. Now, I'm no more happy about this than you are, but it is a fact, so open the damned gate and let me in!"

It all made sense at that very moment. Jolene's mama had told her she was going to get a surprise one day, so here it was, and sure enough it had come right down Hill Road like Mama had said, but it was nothing like she had imagined. In fact, this definitely was not what she hoped it would be. That hope, like all the rest, got dashed against the barbed-wire fence. All this time she had been watching the cemetery, waiting for Mama to tell her what the surprise was. Now it was staring her in the face.

Jolene looked square at that woman and studied her from one end to the other before she walked out and unlatched the gate. She saw it right then. The nose—Pappy's nose, right there in front of her. No mistake, that snooty woman was Pappy's sprout. She had his nose anyhow, and that nose was recognizable anywhere; after all, Jolene saw that nose every morning when she looked in the cracked mirror. That nose and the black eyes stood out like buzzards in the sunshine against that bleached blonde hair with black roots showing.

The woman looked around anxiously as the gate swung open. "Where's Barkley?"

"Over yonder under that tree."

"Where? I don't see him," the woman said, craning her neck nervously.

"*Under* the tree, not beside it. We buried him five years ago," Jolene said. She never cracked a smile.

The woman laughed. "He's dead?" she asked.

"As a door nail," Jolene replied.

"You threatened me with a dead dog?" Finally the stiff mask on her face broke. She laughed until Jolene thought she might pee in her pants.

"Jolene, you really aren't what I thought you'd be," the woman said.

"Well, fancy that. What was I supposed to be?"

"Uhhh, like me," the woman replied.

Jolene looked up at the bright summer sky and said, "Thank you, Jesus! So what did you come to bring me?"

"Well, may I come inside first? Even if there is not a drink of water forthcoming, I'd still appreciate being able to come in out of the heat," said Miss Van Arbuckle.

"I reckon you can, but it ain't much cooler inside. It is June. This is Florida."

The inside of the house wasn't much cooler than the dusty road, but it was at least out of the sun. The woman looked at Jolene and said, "Your father was also my father, but my mother didn't reveal that fact to me until she was on her death bed. She made me promise to visit you and bring this to you." Then she fished in her Gucci handbag and pulled out a small leather pouch.

Jolene held out her hand, and the woman laid the pouch in her open palm. She stood there holding the bag as she twisted her lips to one side and tried to decide whether to open it. "What's in the bag?"

"I have no earthly idea. My mother made me promise to give it to you, and I have. She said you might have knowledge of the contents. Now if you'll excuse me, I'll see myself out." The dark room smelled of dust and old linens, but something familiar about it made her hesitate.

"Now, wait just a minute, Sister! You ain't going nowhere until we see what's in this bag."

"Sister, I might be, but happy, I am not. Goodbye!"

"I'm not exactly thrilled, myself, but it looks to me like the sister part might be true, so cool your britches and sit yourself down."

The woman hesitated and asked, "And what makes you think the sister part is true?"

"Look at that picture hanging on the wall over the settee."

The woman walked over to Pappy's picture and stared at it. "Oh, I see." Her eyebrows stretched so high, Jolene thought they'd meet her hairline.

"Now, sit your bony ass down while we see what's in this bag."

The woman did as she was told. She was no longer in control. Jolene sat across the table from Miss Van Arbuckle and pulled the drawstrings loose. She held the bag upside down and shook it. Four small, perfectly chiseled flint arrowheads slid out. Both of the women laughed. Jolene gave the bag one more shake and out came a small clay box.

"That's all—that's your legacy?" the woman asked.

"Looks that way. Let me show you something," Jolene reached behind her and pulled out the drawer of the pie safe. Inside were several leather pouches identical to the one the woman brought. She set them on the table and said, "Open them, Miss Fancy Britches."

The pie safe intrigued Miss Van Arbuckle. Its front was not glass but some sort of homemade lattice backed by what looked like the inside of a rabbit cage—coarse wire, sturdy but not particularly decorative. Inside she could see three cracked bowls and a mismatched set of glasses in four different colors.

The confused woman turned her attention back to Jolene and opened the first bag. She dumped the contents on the table beside the others. They matched the darkest of the arrow heads in the first pouch. The next and the next also matched others in the pouch. Then she reached back in the pie safe and took out a little clay box.

Jolene grinned when she saw the expression on her sister's face. "Bet you wonder where all these relics came from, don't you?"

"I sure do. Was your father a Native American?"

"Our father, Sister! He's *our* father, not just mine, and yes, he was a Seminole. But he didn't make these arrowheads. He knew where the mound was down by the creek, so we used to go down there and dig for them when I was a kid. I can take you down there if you want me to." The image of this fancy woman climbing in the mud on the creek bank almost made Jolene laugh out loud.

"What's in the clay boxes?"

Jolene opened the first of the boxes to expose two rows of six cells that looked like a honeycomb. Each one contained a perfectly round pearl. The pearls varied from a silver white to slate, and one was as black as onyx.

Miss Van Arbuckle gasped and said, "Do you know what those are?"

"They're pearls out of oysters! Of course I know what they are," Jolene replied.

"But do you know what they are probably worth?"

"Don't matter," said Jolene. "They belonged to Pappy's people. He didn't find them here where he found the arrowheads. His daddy gave them to him. He wanted to make Mama a necklace with them after I was born, but she didn't want them."

Miss Van Arbuckle sat across the table staring at her new-found sister. Finally she slapped the table and said, "I've spent my whole damned life thinking I was a supposed to be *somebody*! What a joke—I never wanted to be anybody but who I am. And I always hated being an only child. I used to pretend I had a sister, but she sure wasn't like you. I didn't have *that* much imagination. Sometimes real is even better than pretend."

Jolene's façade broke. The straightness of her spine relaxed. She took a deep breath. "Mama was right when she told me I'd get a big surprise one day. I never had a sister before, and I sure wouldn't have thought she be like you. What is your name, anyway?"

"Fannie! Just plain, Fannie!"

"Looks to me like you and me are two buzzards in the same cedar tree," said Jolene.

"I reckon so," replied Fannie.

The two of them became sisters that night.

When Jolene woke the next morning, she heard the unfamiliar sound of shuffling feet and the clink of a spoon on the lip of a cup. Fannie had slept in Mama's bed in the little room right next to Jolene's.

When Jolene walked into the tiny kitchen, Fannie was singing softly to herself as she stood in front of the window sipping coffee from a chipped, mostly white cup. She stopped singing and turned around when she heard the soft pad of Jolene's bare feet on the old pine floorboards. She took the pot off the stove and smiled as she poured a cup of coffee for her sister.

Jolene's hair was tied back in one long braid slung across her shoulder. Her face showed her shock when Fannie offered her the cup. "I never had anybody fix my coffee for me before," she said.

"I never fixed coffee for anybody either, so I guess that makes us even. Jolene, let's sit on the front porch and be sisters in the morning sun," she said.

"Do you reckon we know how to do that? I always sit on the porch in the morning, but now I don't need to watch the road anymore. My surprise is right here in my kitchen," Jolene said.

"I'm bettin' we can learn. Being sisters can't be that hard," replied Fannie.

Jolene watched Fannie as she picked up her cup. When Fannie drove up Hill Road the first time, her blonde hair was wrapped into a stern French twist and secured tightly with bronze bobby pins. Not one hair was free from its restraint, but now her hair flopped across her shoulders as she walked. It looked a little like dried, yellow straw, but Jolene thought it was pretty.

Fannie picked up the morning paper from the front steps and stripped off the red rubber band holding it together. She sat down in the old porch swing and gathered her hair at the nape of her neck. Without thinking she slipped the red rubber band around her hair as if she had done it a thousand times before. Jolene bet she hadn't, but still every movement seemed like an old ritual.

Jolene sat down beside her and chuckled. The swing creaked as four feet pushed it forward in a familiar rhythm.

"What's funny?" asked Fannie, looking askance at her sister.

"Oh, nothing. It's just that you look so different today."

"What do you mean? Aside from the fact that I am now wearing your shirt. And I must admit I quite like it, Sister."

"That's actually Pappy's shirt. I think he's ok with you wearing it. I don't want to hurt your feelings, but you didn't exactly come off as friendly yesterday, you know."

"Well, what about you? Threatening me with a dead dog! Now was that friendly?"

"What do you expect? Some hoity toity broad in a Cadillac comes waltzing up to my steps demanding an audience. You'd think I was the Pope or something. And those sunglasses…could you have found a bigger pair?"

"I seriously doubt anyone ever thought of you as the Pope," said Fannie. She looked so different with laugh lines forming on her face.

"Now, how do you know that? You might be surprised at what folks think of me. I just might be the local religious guru."

"In a pig's eye, you are," retorted Fannie.

"Well, don't get too comfortable with that notion, sister. I just might surprise you yet."

"No doubt about that. I've been surprised more in the last twenty-four hours than in all the rest of my life put together. Suddenly, I have no earthly idea who I am or where I came from. I have enough questions to keep you busy till you lie down across the road in one of those stone beds," said Fannie.

"Come to think of it, I got a few questions myself." Jolene pursed her lips and stared across the road at the three marble slabs under the big cedar tree. The buzzards hadn't arrived yet and the dew was still on the spider webs. Both women were quiet. The silence was broken by the scratchy caws of crows circling above and soft lowing from a few cows that needed milking over at the Thompson farm.

After a long silence, Fannie said, "Jolene, I've never felt like I belonged in my world, but suddenly I think I see where I belong. I never had a brother or a sister. I never really had anyone. I don't even think my mama and daddy had anyone, at least not that I could see. They had *stuff*, but they didn't have anyone. They gave me anything I asked for, but I never really thought they wanted me. I didn't know why. They weren't mean to me. I just wasn't there. Now, I suppose I know why they didn't want me, or at least why my daddy didn't want me. I guess neither one of my daddies wanted me."

Jolene became a little girl again, a little girl with a sister, someone who belonged to her, someone to be protected. "I'm sorry, Fanny. At least my daddy always wanted me, and I think my mama loved me too. I always thought they didn't love each other, but they both seemed to love me" she said.

"What was our daddy like? What would it have been like to be your sister?"

"You were my sister," Jolene answered, but when she said the words, something changed in her face and she began to cry. No one other than Barkley had ever seen her cry, not even at her daddy's funeral. Fannie was her sister, so it didn't matter.

"Heavens to Betsy, Jolene! What's wrong with you?" asked Fannie as she put her arms around her sister.

Jolene went limp against Fannie's shoulder and sobbed herself dry. Fannie said nothing but kept rocking her sister in her arms and pushing that old swing by herself.

When the tears dried, Jolene opened her eyes and looked into the sweetest face she had ever seen. It was her sister, a sister who instinctively loved her. Fannie pulled out a neatly folded tissue tucked into her bra and handed it to Jolene. She smiled softly and said, "Dear sister tell me your story. I want to know."

Jolene stared into Fannie's face and began. Fannie patted her hand like she was a child. Lost years faded into memory and they were sisters.

"I was born in this house thirty-four years ago in August," said Jolene.

"Oh my, so was I! Well, not in this house, but I'll be thirty-four in August, too. I guess our daddy was a busy fellow," Fannie replied.

"I guess so. Mama must have found out. That explains why they never slept in the same room."

"Jolene, what kind of car did your daddy have when you were a little girl?" Fannie asked. She wrinkled her brow and puckered her lips.

Jolene hesitated then said, "He didn't have a car, he had an old Ford pickup truck, a black one."

"Hah! That explains it!"

"Explains what?"

"When I was about five years old, I was riding my tricycle on the sidewalk in front of my house. We had a big old white house on a hill. It had columns and wisteria and all that stuff. Mama wanted to live at Tara, so daddy gave her Tara. Anyway, a man in an old black Ford truck pulled up beside the sidewalk and asked me what my name was. He was very nice and got out and gave me a piece of candy. He told me I was pretty, then my daddy came running out of the house with a double-barreled shotgun and pointed it at the man. He told me to go back up to the house. I heard him tell the man if he ever came back, he would kill him. Daddy snatched me up and took me back in the house, but I looked over his shoulder and watched the man drive off. He nearly ran into a ditch because he was leaning out the window to look at me."

"What did your mama say?" asked Jolene.

"Mama was peeking through the curtains. She didn't say anything. Daddy told me to go up to my room. I did, but I could hear him yelling at Mama. He didn't speak to her again for a week. I had no idea why he was so mad at the man until now. That was our daddy. I'd bet my best hat on it."

"No doubt about it, Fannie. He was a good daddy. You would have liked him. I bet he loved you too, but there wasn't any way for him to know you. I wonder if he was in love with your mama."

"Mama was a rounder—that's what folks say. She was beautiful and she wasn't afraid to flaunt it. She always wanted me to be like that. I think I was a big disappointment to her.

I never cared much about bars and flirting with men, and I didn't like to wear fancy dresses. I never realized how much of me was a reaction to her. I didn't want to be like her. She's the one who bought me that old Cadillac. She made me drive a Cadillac when I was in high school. I wanted a cool car like the other kids, but she insisted I drive an *appropriate* car for my station. She believed we were better than everybody else. She made me wear those stupid high heels—even to school. She thought money meant something. I think Daddy bought her then couldn't find the receipt to return her when he realized what he had. I reckon she was Snopes blood and Daddy was Colonel Sartoris," said Fannie.

"What on Earth are you talking about, Sister?"

Fannie laughed. "Oh, nothing. It's a family in a Faulkner story. A Southern trash story. Daddy was like Colonel Sartoris. He had money and good breeding, but not the best judgment when it came to women. Mama had the good looks and charm, but not much breeding. I didn't get the good looks, and I sure couldn't get Daddy's good breeding, so I don't know who I am."

"Mama was a good woman, and Daddy was a good man, but he liked the ladies. He was a looker just like your mama. I reckon that's how you got here. So here we are—two buzzards in a cedar tree! Swing, sister, swing! We found the truth and we found each other. That's enough for me." The old porch swing squeaked and found its rhythm.

"Jolene, was that plate on the table for me?"

"Maybe." Jolene smiled and the swing continued its rhythm.

"Sister, do you reckon our daddy's been looking over us

all along? I bet he left the little bag of arrow heads so we would find each other. Maybe he knew we would need each other. Do you think maybe he really did love me?"

"I'm sure of it, Sister. I remember one time when he came home in that old black truck. He'd been gone all day, and when he came back, he went out to the barn and stayed there till after dark. When he came in, his eyes were red, and Mama gave him one of those nasty looks. She said, 'You been up there again, ain't you?' I bet that's when he went to see you. Sometimes he'd look at me for a long time and be sad. I thought I was doing something wrong, but I think he was just wishing he had both of us. He was a good daddy. You would have loved him, and I'm sure he loved both of his girls. How about we go across the road and visit him?"

You've Got His Hands

James D. Brewer

In the mid-1990s, I was traveling in Tennessee to research an upcoming novel when a long-delayed confrontation tested my spirit. I had recently discovered that my absentee father was living in a small town near the route of the day's research.

I slowed my car as I approached a fork in the highway ahead. A right turn would take me perhaps thirty or forty-five minutes out of the way to the town where my father was living. If I continued straight ahead, I would remain on-task for my day's work. Something told me that after more than forty years I needed to make that turn. As a retired Army officer, I had the skills to find him, so I figured it was time to confront him. After all, he had mistreated me and my mother, such that she threw him out when I was only a few months old. He had abandoned her to raise me by herself. The man was a worthless drunk and he had it coming.

Throughout my life, my only contact with my father had been an occasional phone call at Christmas, perhaps three or four times, during my youth. He was usually drunk when calling, and Mother resisted putting me on the phone with him, but I suppose she felt she had to. I clearly recall one or two of those conversations filled with promises of things he was never going to do, visits he would never make, and toys or gifts that he would never deliver. He promised me a bicycle one Christmas, and I became convinced he would show up with it.

Mother, unable to stand the disappointment I was certain to face, went out and bought a bicycle. Of course, she had to finance it, given we were broke much of the time. And as she often did, she worked overtime hours at the telephone company, sold sandwiches in the breakroom, and made and sold crafts to pull together the extra money. And on Christmas Day I had a new bicycle. I only found out years later that my worthless father had nothing to do with my joy that day.

So here I was, laying aside my plans for the morning to seek some justice. And the farther I drove the angrier I got. Oh, trust me, I had been plenty angry over the years. Several of my friends' fathers had kindly included me in some of their family activities. I so envied that they had a father present and active in their life. But the more I recalled, and the closer I got to the town, the more disgusted I became. He had never seen me play a Little League game. Never been around for advice on a prom date. Never taught me to drive a car. Never saw me graduate from any school. Never met my wife. Never saw his grandchildren. Never saw me successful in my job.

I was not exactly sure what I was going to do when I found him, but I had some ideas. Maybe I would verbally rip him a new one. I would tell him how his actions and lack of caring had hurt me and made it so hard on Mother. Maybe I would curse him. Maybe I would toss him across the room, slap him around a little, and demand to know what kind of worthless, uncaring, demented, booze-guzzling fool would treat his son this way.

After perhaps an hour of detective work, I located where he lived. It was late morning when I parked my vehicle across the street from his house. I sat there for several minutes, calculating my play and eyeing the dilapidated, subsidized, government housing unit that bore the beast. Part of me hoped he would give me some crap. Part of me hoped he would say or do something to give me the excuse to exact some pain from him like he had from me for all those years. The disappointment of my youth, which had boiled into anger as an adolescent, had cooked down into apathy-soup for the better part of my adult life. But this morning that rage was palpable. I sat there for several moments.

Do you really want to do this? Do you really want to open this can of worms?

I told myself I could drive away right now and no one would be the wiser. Instead, I began taking several deep breaths, dug deep for some resolve, opened the car door, walked across the street, and stepped up on the shallow porch.

You can still turn around right now and leave. Who knows, maybe he's not even home.

I knocked on the door.

First, I heard some shuffling about inside, and then the door opened only a few inches. I struggled to see into the room.

"Excuse me," I said. "Can you help me find someone that

lives in this area?"

Releasing the chain latch and cautiously opening the door, a gray-haired, frail-looking old man wearing a housecoat and sporting a two-day growth of beard stood in front me. He appeared weak in his eyes like he had been recently ill, and in those eyes was not a hint of recognition of who was standing before him.

"I'm looking for a Mister...uh...who are you, Sir?

"Brewer," he replied.

It was go-time. I knew I had the right man, and now I had the chance to act.

"I'm looking for a Mister...Caldwell," I told him, fiddling with some papers I had brought along with me as a prop. He shook his head without speaking. "Have you lived here long?" I asked.

"About two years," he said. His voice was weak, and yet I searched my mind for some, or any, familiarity in it.

"Well, I was told he moved in here a few weeks ago," I said, maintaining anonymity. I guess part of me, somewhere deep inside, hoped he would suddenly say 'don't I know you,' or he might somehow miraculously realize who I was. But there was nothing.

"I don't know a Caldwell," he said, staring at me impatiently. I glanced into the room and could see behind him a small table that held three or four prescription medicine bottles. Now was the time for me to tell him who I was. I should announce in grand fashion that I was his long-lost son. I should demand he talk to me. After all, I deserved to know how in the world he could have been so mean and uncaring. He would now, finally, tell me why he preferred alcohol over me and my mother. Seconds crawled by like minutes as I gathered myself for the confrontation. But a voice inside me said, "Wait."

You see, I needed him to be an ogre. I needed him to be loud, demanding, threatening, or maybe even drunk—any kind of trigger that would launch my long-awaited tirade. Instead, what I saw in front of me was a tired, sick, weak old man living alone. I was observing a man who had run off just about everyone in his life that cared anything about him. His behavioral choices had destroyed his body, and now his life was devoid of anyone or anything that mattered. How could it possibly help me or anyone else to launch into a man who was sitting around alone waiting to die? After all, he's the one who missed out, not me. He missed my childhood. He missed the baseball and the football and the growing up. He missed the prom. He missed my wedding. He missed his grandchildren. I was there for all of it. If anyone was the loser here, the loser was standing in front of me.

I had been staring at him now for several moments when he finally said, "What else can I do for you?"

"Nothing," I replied. "There's absolutely nothing you can do for me."

I turned around, stepped off the porch, and walked to my car without looking back. I drove away that day, my mind a jumble of thoughts, not the least of which was whether I had done the right thing. Maybe I should have dressed him down. Maybe I should have kicked his ass. Many years have now passed, and I am since satisfied with my choice that day.

But for all that my father didn't do in my life, I must

admit that he taught me something even in his absence. I learned that I wanted to always be a part of my children's lives, so I made sure I was there for the ball games and the graduations and the proms. I learned that I never wanted to allow alcohol or anything else to become more important than my family. I learned that even someone we despise is capable of being loved by someone else. My mother loved him—she just knew she couldn't live with him. And the fact that she never spoke badly about him showed grace, and I learned that the longer I carried this resentment the longer it would drag me down.

I heard that my father died about a year after that encounter, and at my wife's urging I attended the funeral. Maybe I was seeking the ever-popular word "closure." No more than a handful of people showed up, and it appeared that the minister had been the on-call chaplain or something because he seemed to know very little about anyone gathered there. Three half-sisters by my father's later re-marriage showed up, along with my father's brother. I tried to be gracious to those in attendance, but I spoke very little. After some generic remarks by the minister, I walked up to the casket with my wife by my side. Digging deep for my own indomitable spirit, I studied his face as he lay in repose, thinking to myself that this will, at last, close a sad chapter in my life.

Then my wife leaned past me, pointed to the body, and said, "Look, Jim, you've got his hands."

A tear crept down my cheek. I wiped it away quickly and that was that.

Searching for Dad

Nancy Holder Pressley

"What a terrible way to spend this nice spring day," Naomi thought as she clutched her hand and tried valiantly to control her urge to cry out in pain. When her mother closed the back door of their car, Naomi's left hand got caught just above the knuckles. At first, her hand was simply numb, but the throbbing level of pain was becoming difficult to bear in silence.

Entering the funeral home with her younger brother by her side and their mother leading the way, Naomi felt out of place. At age fifteen, this would be her first funeral.

Naomi and Justin were greeted by family members they had not seen in the eight years since moving out of the city to live in their grandparents' home. It was more than obvious that their mother, Mira, was not offered the same friendly welcome.

Mira brought her two children to the front of the chapel. They passed by their father's open coffin, where they saw his lifeless body. After pausing for a brief time, Naomi's family sat on the left side of the chapel to wait for the service.

Other than a few people telling Naomi that she looked like her father, there was only one memorable moment. Her

Grandmother Peters ran over to the coffin and grabbed her son's torso while wailing, "He was all alone when he died with no one to look after him."

The official cause of death according to the medical examiner was cardiac arrest. Grandmother Peters preferred to cite that document as the whole truth. It would have been embarrassing to add that he could not retain a job due to his alcohol addiction, that he was not able to support his family, and that his anger resulted in frequent outbursts of violence. She did not refer to the fact that his body was found in a ditch some distance from home.

In retrospect, his mother's accusation against Mira was a way of transferring guilt. She may have actually known that Mira was right in making the hard decision in 1950 to move her children to a more stable environment.

The next day, a Wednesday, Naomi returned to school. It was a high school requirement to stop at the attendance office with an excuse for any absence before entering classes. As she explained to the clerk that she had attended her father's funeral, she received a puzzled look. *"I guess I didn't look sad enough for her,"* Naomi thought.

Later that day and in many subsequent reflective moments, she asked herself, *"How should I have acted? How should I feel about the death of my father? Perhaps I should feel relieved. At least now I don't have to be embarrassed when people ask me about my father. Where does he work? Can he come to this or that event? Does he read your report cards? Is he proud of the pictures you draw and paint?"*

Her mother, Mira, was not forthcoming with family history. Asking her anything was like pulling teeth. By nature, Mira was introverted and seemed uncomfortable talking about herself or anything involving her past. In the absence of valid information, Naomi relied on her own limited memories and her imagination.

What did she really know about Justin Peters Sr.? She had been told that he was married at least once before marrying her mother. There were two children born to that previous union, a boy and a girl. This meant that Naomi had half-siblings that she had never met.

She knew her father had served in the Navy during the last part of World War II. She knew this mostly from old photographs of him wearing his uniform and holding her and her brother. Nobody informed Naomi about her father's enlistment—whether he joined voluntarily or was drafted—and his stationing, leaving her with limited information. She could not remember him or her mother ever discussing the Navy.

She knew Mira's friend Patsy had introduced her parents. Her maternal grandmother informed her about that minor detail and seemed to blame all the negative results of their union on poor Patsy.

According to her mother, Justin Sr. had worked as a glazer, installing plate-glass windows and panels for a construction company in the Washington, D.C. area. To be more accurate, that is what he did *when* he was working. At some point, he had created a mirror which hung in the living area. The unusual design would later remind Naomi of the Art Deco period. Years later, she wondered what became of that mirror.

Vague memories of what he said and did during her early years gave Naomi the rest of her impressions. The comment he made to her during a brief visit when she was twelve remained forever etched into her brain and continued to undermine her self-image.

Naomi's memories of their lives together in the city included small snatches or mind pictures and moments in time. She recalled seeing a taxi driver deliver a bottle of Four Roses liquor to the house.

She remembered returning from a visit to their grandparents to find her little black kitten *gone*. Another time, her parakeet lay strangled on the floor of his cage. Someone had thrown her dollhouse across the room with all the interior furnishings destroyed.

One afternoon, she came home from school and saw her mother bandaging her father's hand and cleaning up broken glass. He was in a bad mood and taken his anger out on a bathroom window on the lower floor of the house. Her little brother had witnessed the event and was hiding.

The move in 1950 to a residential community across the Potomac River from D.C. remained fuzzy in Naomi's mind. Her mother never explained what was happening, and Naomi and Justin never questioned it. Since they had begun their lives in their grandparents' home in northeast Washington and had visited them several times after they had moved out, it did not seem strange. They probably never considered that it be a permanent move. Adults in the early 1950s did not expect children to question their decisions. Naomi and Justin did not ask why their father did not move with them.

There was so much in their new environment requiring adjustments. Naomi and Justin explored the neighborhood, made friends, and played freely. It was warm weather and they spent most of the days outside.

One thing Naomi did notice was the mostly nuclear families within her four- to six-block exploration area. Most households were comprised of a mother and a father, plus two or more children.

She did not dwell on that difference; however, she could not think of a suitable answer when a new friend asked about her father. Sometimes she said, "He works in the city." Much later, she learned her parents were legally separated. Most people in the 1950s saw divorce as a disgrace, and Naomi was unsure whether separation had any less of a stigma.

Children of elementary school ages rarely pay attention to the burdens or disappointments of the adults who care about them. They are too busy learning about the world and finding additional sources of entertainment.

As an adult, Naomi realized the sacrifices her mother and grandparents had made to provide her and Justin with basic needs and education. Looking back on it, she also realized that her mother was a young woman at the time and gave up any chance for a different future out of duty.

Mira was an intelligent woman, but she had dropped out of high school after the tenth grade. The lack of a diploma barred her from many job openings in the metropolitan area. For the first few years, she provided childcare for her brother's two children. With the help of the next-door neighbor, she eventually found a job with a government contractor in their printing department. She kept this position until she retired twenty-five years later.

If Mira had a plan for what she would do after the separation, she did not share that with her children. As it was, her job allowed her to contribute to the household expenses and to provide her two children with the essentials. That was not everything they wanted, but certainly what they needed.

Naomi learned much later there was never any monetary child support from their father. After his death, Mira received a small amount of social security from his account until each child reached eighteen. For Naomi, that was two and a half years. For Justin, five.

The beginning of the school year in September 1950 was another change for the two Peters siblings. Naomi was entering the third grade and Justin would be a first grader three months prior to his sixth birthday. He was not emotionally ready, but the age requirement for eligibility at the time was six years of age at any point in the school year.

When Naomi was first enrolled in kindergarten in the city, her mother walked her to school every day. In first and second grades, she was permitted to walk with a neighborhood friend who was the same age. The school was a short three- or four-block walk from home. The high school had been partially renovated to accommodate the elementary overflow, but everything was too oversized for young kids. The locker-filled halls and high toilets and water fountains were intimidating.

Arlington County, VA, provided bus services for students who lived more than a mile away from the assigned school. Naomi and Justin did not qualify, so Naomi took responsibility for leading her brother in the right direction during his first year of school. Fortunately, they walked as a group with neighborhood friends. They knew a few of their new classmates; however, there were many unfamiliar faces in their rooms. Part of the first day's routine was the process of introductions. As each child was asked to tell who they were and something about themselves and their families, Naomi gritted her teeth. *"Here we go again with questions I would prefer to avoid. Think fast."*

When her turn came, she stood up and said, "My name is Naomi Peters and my brother, Justin and I, just moved here from the city in the spring. It is Justin's first year, and I helped him find the way." Quickly sitting down, she hoped that there would be no follow up, at least today. Naturally, there was more informal conversation during recess and lunchtime.

Naomi had learned early that she could avoid personal questions by turning the conversation back to the other person. People love to talk about themselves. If you give them the chance, they will monopolize all the allotted talking time.

The third grade in Arlington County Schools went well for Naomi. She continued to be in the highest reading group, just as she was in first and second grades. Her artwork found favor with students and teachers. She enjoyed friendships with several classmates.

Life was not as happy for Justin. He was struggling and homesick. Several times that year, Naomi was called out of her class to sit with him because he was upset.

The next year, their neighborhood was assigned to a different elementary school. This happened several additional times before they moved into junior high school. Apparently, the county was undergoing a redistricting process, and no one wanted them in their district. That sounds like a bit of paranoia but is emblematic of how the neighborhood felt. Having to change schools every year meant being the new kids repeatedly. Naomi realized that other new students also struggled with feeling awkward, but her extreme introversion increased the discomfort and caused her to turn more to her internal resources.

Children develop part of their personal identities from their close family relationships. Parents and sometimes grandparents become role models of behavior and of aspirations. Boys look to their fathers and girls to their mothers for direction and training in their historical roles. They also look to their parents of the opposite gender for affirmation of their worth. When one of those models is missing, children look at the next likely examples.

Naomi could recall zero positive feedback from her father. The last words from his mouth to her were, "Stand up straight and hold your stomach in."

In her generous moments, she would decide that he was simply helping her to think about posture so that she might feel more confident. In less generous times, she decided he was telling her, *"You are not pretty. I am ashamed to be seen with you."*

Naomi never shared these feelings of deep hurt with her mother. Her family unit was not big on discussing feelings. That was most likely the norm for the Greatest Generation into which her parents and grandparents were born. They had survived great hardships and learned to suck it up and move on.

Her own age group is now referred to as the Silent Generation. If she had entered this world only five years later, she could have felt free to "let it all hang out" with the Baby Boomers.

From a more adult point of view, Naomi explained that the absence of any demonstrative affection from her mother had been assimilated from her culture of toughness and duty. Love was expressed in actions instead of words, hugs, or kisses.

Talking with her brother later in life, Naomi learned that neither of them could remember their mother ever saying, "I love you." They both felt certain that she did love them but was unable to express her feelings in words.

For Naomi, the logical next father figure from whom she could take clues was her grandfather. Fred Banks was a gentleman of the southern tradition. Leaving a family farm to find work in the city, he held several low-level positions before becoming a debit salesperson for a life insurance company. He continued to work in that job until retirement, even after moving out of the city.

Unlike his city residence, life in the suburbs gave him the opportunity to have a vegetable garden and to plant flowers. Naomi imagined it reminded him of his youth in the country. Fred genuinely liked people. He enjoyed talking with his clients of several ethnic groups. He made friends with neighbors in this more open environment.

During his marriage to Naomi's grandmother, Fred had opened his doors to several of her siblings when they needed shelter. And now he was once again sharing his small space and limited income with his daughter and grandchildren. If he held any resentment related to this intrusion, he never expressed it in any way.

To Naomi, her grandfather was a steady source of comfort and entertainment. Fred encouraged both Naomi and Justin to work with him in the garden at whatever level of capability they possessed. Watching plants grow and harvesting their own food was a learning opportunity for his grandchildren.

Fred taught them to play checkers, dominos, and cards. He bought a set of encyclopedias for them to use for school reference work. He took them on company outings where they observed and even tried fishing. In summary, Naomi saw how a male head of household not only provided for his family but also spent personal time with them.

Two other father figures within her extended family displayed attachments to their daughters that Naomi had never enjoyed. Her uncle James was over the moon with joy when his little girl arrived on the scene. Professional photographers caught her charms on large canvas portraits and James arranged for her to appear on a local morning television show featuring beautiful babies. Her great-uncle Henry constantly bragged about his daughter as she finished her nursing degree, and he gave her a lavish wedding. Naomi was overwhelmed as she attended that beautiful outdoor celebration and dreamed of something similar for herself, knowing that would probably never happen to her.

Next in line as a role model was the pastor at the Baptist Church she began attending with her mother and brother shortly after the move to Arlington. Reverand Stevenson was handsome, intelligent, compassionate with children of all ages, and a source of sage advice. The pastor became a substitute father for many children during his years of service. He encouraged Naomi to participate in a speech contest and coached her through the process. She began to look at her pastor as an ideal man and father figure. His influence helped Naomi to gradually develop the confidence to speak up, at least in situations where she felt safe.

When a boy at church, several years her senior, invited her to a ball game, she felt a surprise validation of having some worth. She and Dave dated for a year, during which he gave her his class ring to wear.

Naomi visited Dave's home on several occasions and observed a well-functioning, intact family unit. It was apparent that Dave learned his manners and people skills from his parents, especially his father.

In junior high school, Naomi was still very reserved and reluctant to put herself forward until a few teachers praised her for her performance. A social studies instructor took her aside one day and told her she should plan on college. When Naomi mentioned not being able to afford a college education but that she was planning on secretarial school, she was advised to plan for both possibilities. With that encouragement, she elected several college preparatory courses and a mixture of business subjects.

Several high school teachers gave her encouragement, but she retained a natural introverted nature. It didn't boost her ego to observe that many of the students with whom she had classes were children of high-level government employees and other professional occupations. They all had the latest clothing and drove new cars to school every day. Naomi, of course, rode the bus and worked at a department store part time to buy a few clothes in the current styles. Her mother had made most of her clothing from the time she was small until Naomi began sewing. Still today, she often makes outfits for herself.

As fate would have it, a special government grant became available during Naomi's senior year. There was a national teacher shortage, and the grant was a four-year college subsidy in return for ten years of public-school teaching. This made it possible for Naomi to revise her plans and make applications to colleges. Although she thought she would be starting this new adventure with her best friend, that was not to be. Thus, Naomi completed the enrollment process and entered her freshman class alone before her eighteenth birthday.

Naomi suddenly realized when her mother and brother dropped her off at the campus that she would be attending school twelve hours by car from the only area of the country she had ever known. Most college students visit potential schools before making their decision. There was no one in her family to lead her through the normal initiation steps, so here was Naomi, on her own in a strange place, with no friends, and in a very different local culture. Although her natural reticence and fragile ego made Naomi reluctant to try new challenges or meet new people, she gradually stiffened her spine and learned to step out into opportunities.

College was a decisive improvement for Naomi's development of self. It was in that environment that she explored new world views and new methods of thinking, made friends out of strangers, dated several students, and met the man who would later become her husband. Little by little, she realized that she had greater potential than she had ever believed.

Although her career was not exactly what she had earlier expected, she successfully handled each fork in the winding path. The first third of her public work was spent as a social worker. The last two thirds involved human resource management and consulting. In each phase she was promoted to positions of responsibility.

Her multi-faceted forty-five year career required forcing herself to take on public speaking, management, program development, and to make uncomfortable decisions. After completing some of the larger projects, she would ask herself, *"Did I actually do that?"*

Naomi did not devote much of her time to commiserating about her unfortunate relationship with her father; however, she would still occasionally wonder, *"What would he think of me now?"*

In her graduate school studies, Naomi read and heard more than once that children form their basic ability to bond with people and build trust through their parental interactions. If it does not happen during that early period, it is very difficult to develop a solid level of trust later. Based on that theory, Naomi wondered whether her own ability to trust had been permanently damaged. Was she able to trust anyone totally, especially men? Would she always be expecting to be disappointed and deserted. Did she need to maintain a protective shell and never allow herself to reveal her deepest feelings or thoughts? Could she accept compliments about herself or praise for her work without expecting an ulterior motive?

Then she would catch herself and laugh. *"Cut it out! No*

one is plotting against you. In fact, it is doubtful that anyone is giving you half of the time thinking about you that you spend obsessing. Get over yourself! Do something productive. Remember what your favorite aunt told you: The way to be happy is to work at making someone else happy."

***

In the fourth quarter of her life, Naomi began re-evaluating her personal history—the ups and downs, achievements, and disappointments. When she decided to write a memoir for her daughter, many of the old feelings about her father or the lack thereof ran like an old newsreel through her mind. She was surprised and angry at herself for still harboring those long-buried feelings of betrayal and abandonment. *"Get over it for heaven's sake, you are seventy plus years old,"* she berated herself.

It was at that moment Naomi decided to write a letter to her father in which she hoped to vent all her emotions for a final time.

Mr. Justin Peters Sr.,

I thought I would reach out to you with an update on the daughter you never really tried to know. For many years, I blamed myself for being unworthy of your attention or affection. I was convinced that I was not good enough to make you want to be a father to me or my brother. Looking at early photos of Justin Jr. and myself, I saw two very attractive young children. Justin had your blond hair and I had auburn-brown ringlets like Shirley Temple. Back then, the only reason I could deduce for your lack of caring in my younger mind was that we were not loveable.

It took me many years and the kindness of many other people for me to see myself in another way. Now that I know my value, I am forgiving myself for all those years of self-doubt. Not that I expect you to care, but I am also forgiving you. Since you did not allow me to really know you as a father, I can only surmise that you were too occupied with your own demons to have the energy to learn to know us. So, yes, I forgive you and I feel sorry for you.

The only things I wanted from you would have cost you nothing but your time and attention. The only things you gave me were my brother, whom I love dearly, and my frizzy hair, which I have battled for decades.

As I grew up, other people entered my life who affirmed my value and helped me to become what my stunted self-image had prevented earlier. People have encouraged my intellectual, creative, and spiritual growth. People have loved me. Men have found me attractive. I have had an interesting and rewarding life, but by choice you were not involved in any of that. Why do I feel sorry for you? Here are a few of the reasons and some of the moments you missed:

1. Having a sweet young girl climb in your lap and tell you how much she loved her daddy,
2. Congratulating her as she learned to read, draw, sew, and taught herself to type when only twelve,
3. Watching her develop into a young woman,

4. Seeing her cross the stage as a high school graduate (the first in our family),
5. Watching her accept her college diploma (another first),
6. Walking her down the aisle as a lovely bride, and
7. Being proud of her as she became: a loving mother of a beautiful, intelligent, and compassionate daughter (your granddaughter); a County Director of Welfare; a Deputy Director of a Community Action Agency; a commissioner of a local housing authority; a Vice President of Human Resources; a consultant; and a Published Author.

May You Rest in Peace,
Your biological daughter, Naomi

As much as she hated airline travel, Naomi booked a direct flight to Reagan National Airport and hired a taxi for a trip to Arlington National Cemetery. She had directions to the grave where she had watched her father's burial at a military funeral six decades earlier.

Naomi paid the driver to wait for her and return her to the airport. She took the sealed envelope containing her letter and attached it with a piece of duck tape to the back of the white grave marker, identical to thousands of others, in this beautiful and sacred place.

"There, I survived you. I am now over you. God bless your soul," she prayed as she returned to her taxi.

Naomi smiled at everyone she saw all throughout the plane ride home.

Life Turning on a Dime

Vanessa Davis Griggs

"You look just like your daddy," people who knew me and my daddy, James Davis Jr., used to say. It always made me smile. But when I looked at myself in the mirror, I couldn't really see it. It was not until a hurried glance at my expired 1995 driver's license photo, as I was changing it out for my renewed one, did I see the sameness in our faces. I laughed at how much my license picture looked like a long-haired version of my father.

I've forever known my daddy as a hard worker who loved his family. Being the oldest child, I had fourteen months as the only child until my other four siblings began to make their way onto the scene. Daddy has always been a churchgoing, God-fearing man, who seemed to work from the time he woke up until he laid down. My mother and others gleefully loved telling the story of how, two weeks after my birth in 1959, my father (by himself while my mother adhered to the six-week recuperation rule mandated in those days) carried me to church in my "big old white bassinet."

My father worked at Hayes International Aircraft back when it was hard for a black man to be hired by certain companies. Hayes was a great place to work but notorious for (on a dime) laying folks off for long periods of time. During those times, Daddy made sure he was doing some kind of work somewhere to keep money flowing into our household. He was the person that folks in the community and beyond called on to fix whatever was broken or not working properly. Back when no one in our town had running water, he hauled water from a spring for our home and many others in the community. I was a little over six years old when running water finally came to our town.

Daddy built our house. When I say built it, I mean he laid out what he wanted and, with his own two hands (using saws, hammer, nails, etc.), *built* our house. He started off with the basement so we could move from staying at his father's house and have somewhere to live as he added onto the rest of the house. In the very beginning, there were three bedrooms, a living room and dining room combination area, kitchen, hallway, and a small room that was to become a future bathroom. He built an outhouse that had me believing we were rich. You see, unlike other outhouses, ours was a two-seater with a window at the very top that allowed sunlight to flow in.

A few years later, Daddy added onto our house, first finishing that vacant room into a bathroom housing a step-up, large, green marble bathtub with gold fixtures. He then built a den off from the kitchen, a laundry area with a gas hot water heater, and another full bathroom. Eventually, he added a carport off from the kitchen and den. The no-longer-needed outhouse was converted into a storage shed that housed his fishing equipment and work tools.

I remember Daddy teaching me how to nail in the

subfloor in the den. The den had something I'd never seen before: three complete walls that extended from the floor to the ceiling made of double-pane windows with built-in metal blinds between the glass panes that easily opened and shut with their own turn-crank. Daddy was good at creating something from nothing.

Daddy fixed his vehicles when they broke down and did his own oil changes. Every year, he planted a huge garden. Eventually, he bought a tiller. He planted tomatoes, Irish potatoes, sweet potatoes, turnip greens, collard greens, okra, green beans, squash, etc. We had plum trees, strawberries, pear trees, a persimmon tree, a muscadine vine, a peach tree, and a fig tree. I would climb up the plum trees and gently shake them when we wanted more ripe plums to pick. In August, I could be found standing on a yellow rubber strapped lawn chair in the muscadine vine picking grapes. Daddy was a true provider.

When it came to money, my father was a saver. As children he made sure we all had a savings account (our own blue book) and taught us to deposit money into our account (even if it was just a dime). In the beginning, we didn't have a lot of money. When you start out with no passed-down inheritance, it takes a lot longer to build up wealth speed. Unlike my two younger siblings who got a lot of money when they came along, I didn't get an allowance until around my high school years. At one point, Daddy started working the late shift at Hayes so I didn't get to see him until the weekends.

"Daddy, I need thirty-five cents," I said when I saw him and could talk face to face.

He asked what for, and I told him it was for a school event.

"I'll think about it," he said. I was praying he would give it to me or I wouldn't be able to participate, but getting it wasn't a given.

On the day before the final deadline, Daddy hadn't given me the money, meaning I wouldn't be able to participate in the event. I wrote him a note that night and placed it where he would see it when he came home from work during the midnight hour. The next morning, I discovered a quarter and a dime on my note. Seeing those coins made me smile. Something minute to others impacted me so profoundly that over fifty-five years later I still remember it.

Daddy loved to fish. He'd take us fishing with him to Pittman Lake and Higginbotham Lake where he knew the folks who owned these private places but didn't permit everyone to fish from their banks. After the folks he knew were no longer around, his new local spot became Inland Lake. In the beginning, he rented a boat whenever we went up there, which was neat for anyone who had only fished from a bank. Daddy soon bought his own green metal boat he would take when we went, first rowing the boat out into the lake until he eventually bought a motor. He absolutely loved it!

His other favorite activity was deep-sea fishing. In the early days, he and a group of his fishing buddies would leave on a Friday night (most times from Hayes after his shift ended), and they would head down to Florida. He even put a camper on the bed of his red Ford truck so those going could sit on a cushioned bench he made and placed back there for them. After his favorite boat captain died, he started going to Mobile, Alabama. As a rite-of-passage, he took every one of his children (individually) and a few grandchildren deep-sea fishing at least once.

He kept an eight-foot chest freezer filled with fresh-caught red snappers, groupers, and what Daddy called "mother-in-law" (which until I started writing this, I didn't know the actual name was *cabezon*). I loved mother-in-law fish because he would skin it using pliers and fileted it where you didn't have to deal with bones when you ate it. That was what I hated most about eating lake fish—the bones. Locally, he caught brims, bass, and rainbow trout, which were full of tiny bones that, if not careful, can easily get stuck in your throat.

"Here. Eat this piece of bread," Daddy would say should a bone get stuck in our throat.

I've not had a mother-in-law fish in decades. A moratorium was placed on the number of red snappers that could be caught and kept years before Daddy was forced to stop going deep sea fishing altogether. Daddy hated how this was done. People still caught red snappers but, because only five per person (I believe it was) could be kept, Daddy said folks would throw back the smallest ones after multiple catches to retain the largest ones. He believed those thrown back likely didn't survive after being hooked, kept in a cooler, then thrown back just because they didn't make the "size" cut. Daddy was a fisherman but also a fisher of men in his own way.

Seeing all my father did and could do, it's no wonder I was known for saying, "My daddy can do anything!" My baby sister called him our "Superman." He'd grown up having to work while in school to help out his family. His mother died when he was young. They'd found her dead as she nursed her infant son. It was said she'd been poisoned, possibly by her own brother who was feuding with her at the time. Had her infant son not unlatched while nursing, they say he would have died as well. Daddy's father then married a woman who had three boys of her own. Combined with my father and his two brothers, there were now six boys.

Daddy saved Kennedy fifty-cent pieces and what people called "Bo" dollars (slang for a one-dollar silver coin). He soldered a toolbox shut and cut a slot in it to push these large coins through, transforming it into a huge metal bank. It wasn't easy getting money from Daddy. He was tight with his money. As an adult, I remember one day having a need to borrow some money from him. I mustered up my courage, having my pitch ready to hopefully contract a yes.

"How much do you need?" he asked after I made my pained plea.

"800 dollars," I said, with a promise to pay him back in two weeks.

He laughed, then opened his wallet and handed me the requested amount right then and there. "This is my walking around money," he said with a grin.

In that moment, I saw a glimpse of how God thinks of us as His children. My earthly father had it; I just had to ask. It was almost nothing for him as it was his "walking around money." I could hear Matthew 7:11 (KJV) saying, "If ye then, being evil, know how to give good gifts unto your children, how much more shall your Father which is in heaven give good things to them that ask him?" But don't get it twisted. It was hard to get Daddy to give up his money. He didn't play when it came to his hard-earned dimes.

My father was a great baker, making all our cakes using an extensive sour cream pound cake recipe that included several different extracts and apricot nectar. He made all of our birthday cakes as sheet cakes with pink strawberry icing and our name piped on them. He baked regular pound cakes, three-layer caramel icing pound cakes, and three-layer chocolate icing pound cakes. Yearly, he made a fruit cake that was dense (and quite heavy) and lasted (unlike a light fruit cake I now make) from before Christmas to February of the following year.

I remember when Hayes did one of their infamous layoffs and Daddy went to work full-time for B. F. Goodrich. He was there for months before Hayes called him back. Unsure how long before the next layoff cycle might be, Daddy decided to continue working for both companies full-time. That's one reason he chose the late shift at Hayes. That was sixteen work hours (plus travel and lunchtimes with both jobs) done in a twenty-four-hour day. He kept this up for over a year. Never missed a Sunday church service that included at least one two-hour-plus afternoon church program service once a month while also maintaining his garden and other activities.

My father was not perfect, but he was the ultimate example of an honest, hardworking person of integrity. He didn't have a problem telling you what and how he *really* felt. If someone cut him off in traffic when he was driving the car, he would say, "If I was in my truck, I would have run slap over them!" If Daddy didn't like you, he had no problem letting you know. You didn't have to guess or wonder where you stood with him.

There was this guy who wanted to take me shopping. I didn't really want to go, but my mother told me to be nice and go. When we returned to my house, the guy decided he wanted to fuss with me because he wanted me to be his girlfriend, and I let him know I really wasn't interested. He grabbed me by my wrist. I struggled to get loose, but he held even tighter. I told him to let go of me. He then slapped me. In *my* house! I will confess here: that was the one and *only* time a man has *ever* put his hand on me in that way.

Daddy was outside tilling his garden. Even with the tiller blasting, somehow my daddy heard me screaming at this guy (three years my senior) without knowing he had just slapped me. The next thing I knew, Daddy had shut off that tiller, stopped off at his truck, retrieved his .38 pistol, and came bursting in the house. He let that guy know that if he *ever* laid his hand on me again, it would be his last time. This guy was still talking and apologizing to Daddy when I left the house with the man I would end up marrying some years later. To this day, I don't know how Daddy was able to hear me over the loud sound of the tiller and come to my rescue. But, like Superman, he did! Daddy was a protector of those he loved.

On a Sunday morning in May of 2000, my father had a stroke. For a man who was never sick, it was hard seeing him lying in that emergency room bed.

"Mr. Davis, can you squeeze my hand?" the nurse said.

Daddy looked up at her. My mother, sister Danette, and

I knew Daddy well enough to know this wasn't a good thing to ask him to do. He prided himself on being able to squeeze a hand and bring that person to their knees. But he'd had a stroke as he was getting up to get ready for church. My sister and I laughed and told the nurse this wasn't going to end well for her. We knew that would make Daddy laugh, and he did as he squeezed her hand. Not to the level he would have had he not suffered a stroke, but enough to make her smile and encouragingly pat his hand.

He would go through physical therapy and seemed to be on the mend. But in November of that same year, he suffered another stroke. He and I talked at the hospital. I told him I was scheduled to speak at an event in Tuscaloosa, Alabama, that night but he was in the hospital now.

"Vanessa, you go on and do what you need to do. I'll be all right. There's nothing much you can do here. I'm being taken care of. Go on and do what you're on this earth to do," he said as my mother echoed that sentiment.

That's us. That's how I was raised. Keep your word and your commitment. No excuses. So, I went to Tuscaloosa and encouraged an event full of people. I told them what was going on with my father, but that we both agreed just how important they were.

After being released to go home, my father did what he always did on Sundays: he went to church. Shout out to my mother who took such great care of him. His left side was greatly affected by the second stroke. "My arm won't do what I tell it," he said, trying to lift his arm. "I'm telling it, but it won't obey." He worked hard and was able to move enough to stand up from his chair to a wheelchair, but not walk with ease, having to shuffle or to unbend his now stiffened left arm. Eventually, he got a red scooter. We teased him with how it matched his beloved red Ford truck he'd fully restored inside and out a few years before he'd had his stroke.

Daddy's emotions weren't under his control. There were times he would just start to cry while he was talking. In all my years, I'd never seen my daddy cry. He would be laughing at something and the effects from the stroke would cause his laugh to flip into an uncontrollable cry. That was hard for him and, truthfully, for us.

My mother announced she was going to Indiana in November one year to visit relatives. Daddy was so determined he was going to church that he told her he would ride his scooter over there. The house is located on a hill. You have to then cross a four-lane highway just to get to the road to reach the church building. I told him I would come over and take him, but he said he would be all right. I didn't argue with him, but still went. As I drove up to the church, I found myself checking to make sure he hadn't fallen into a ditch.

There were times his birthday would fall on Thanksgiving Day, but that year it was the following Monday. I bought a cake and took it to church so we could sing "Happy Birthday" to him. It was me and him, except I wasn't being carried in a bassinet...just loving on and taking care of him the way he'd loved on and taken care of us. We had so much fun that day!

Daddy's mind was remarkably still sharp following his stroke. I picked up a lot of knowledge from my daddy whether inherited or just watching him while growing up. I am the person who fixes things and can build and assemble. Like Daddy, I instinctively know what to do.

When his left side became hard to move, he still figured out how to do things he loved. He created a small garden on the back patio porch using pots to grow tomatoes and other easily controllable type vegetables. He'd sit outside for hours, enjoying nature. His scooter stopped working one day. Normally, he would have fixed it, but it was difficult with only one working hand. I went over and figured out the wires had fractured and weren't connecting properly. I went and bought electrical tape, cut the wiring, reconnected them, then taped the wires back together. Voila! Fixed! He was rolling again. I saw the pride in his eyes that I could do the things he would have done had he been able.

Daddy started mentally declining around 2017. He became bedridden where he couldn't go to church anymore. Again, my mother was his primary caregiver, which is not an easy job. Anyone who has experienced it knows that many times caregivers and loved ones take the brunt of abuse from those who feel a need to lash out at something or someone.

Daddy had an in-home hospital bed with railings, and he wanted out of it. I was there one day, and he was trying to get me to let the railing down so he could get out. He kept saying, "Vanessa, fix it."

"Fix what, Daddy?" I asked.

He took his hand and brushed it over the railing without telling me exactly what he wanted fixed. After repeatedly asking him what he wanted fixed, I remember just saying, "Okay, Daddy." The next day, he started telling my mother I had lied.

"Lied about what?" I asked Mama. She couldn't tell me because she didn't know.

So, when I got off work, I drove to their house. I walked in and went over to him. "Daddy, what did I lie about?" I asked right off the bat after greeting him.

He looked at me. I repeated the question. He began to smile, and then started chuckling. He was happy to see me. My mother then said, "Oh, you just wanted to get Vanessa over here, didn't you?"

Daddy laughed. I held his hand and said, "I love you, Daddy."

"I love you too, Vanessa." Then his laugh turned into that uncontrolled crying.

Daddy really began to go downhill. His mind was no longer strong. There were signs of dementia. I remember him telling us how he'd driven an airplane up to the house. We tried to tell him he hadn't actually driven it to the house, but most likely he was talking about moving one when he worked at Pemco (formerly Hayes International). He became agitated that we were disagreeing with him and told us in no uncertain terms that he *had* driven an airplane up the hill and parked it on the road down below the house.

On April 30, 2018, I came home from work and called to check on my mother and father. Mama said Daddy had been sleeping pretty much since the nurse, who had been at the house earlier that day to see him, had left. I told her I was coming over; it was around six that evening. She said I could just wait and come after work tomorrow. I don't know what it was, but I told her I was coming over now, and I would be there shortly. I took my husband and oldest son with me, because I felt we all needed to go see him.

When I walked in, Daddy was still sleeping. I didn't want to wake him, but Mama said it was okay because he needed to wake up. She said if he knew I was there, he would wake up and talk. She said loudly, "James, Vanessa is here!" He didn't wake up. "James, Vanessa is here!"

I began talking to him. I touched him. I kissed his forehead. But he wouldn't wake up. My two sisters came. One thing Daddy enjoyed was when we pretended to argue about who was his favorite. So that's what we did. We did it loud enough for him to hear us. My sister Danette, who is fourteen months younger than me, said, "Everybody knows I'm Daddy's favorite."

My sister Arlinda said, "No. Daddy will wake up for me because I'm his favorite."

When Daddy didn't wake up during this, my mother knew what was happening. She then called my two brothers and told them that she wasn't sure how much longer Daddy had, and they might want to come on over. My brother Terence, who is the third child, came right away. My baby brother, Emmanuel, didn't. So, the four of us were trying to get Daddy to open his eyes. He wouldn't. He either couldn't hear us or he could but couldn't make his eyes obey.

At one point I took his hand and held it. "Daddy, if you can hear me, squeeze my hand." Nothing. I said it again. At first nothing, then a gentle squeeze. His breathing was steady, but his eyes remained closed.

I had to be at work at 5 a.m. It was 9:30 p.m. One of the nurses assigned to Daddy had come and called the doctor, who called in a prescription to ensure Daddy wasn't in any pain. I volunteered to go get it, but my sister Arlinda said she would go. Knowing I had to be up early for work, my mother insisted I go home, promising to keep me posted.

After we were in the car, my oldest son, Little Jeffery, told me he'd said, "Bye, Granddaddy." Daddy (with his eyes still closed) had raised his hand up slightly as if to wave goodbye. Normally, Little Jeffery would have shaken Daddy's hand goodbye, but this time he said he didn't. The only one who saw Daddy raise his hand was my son.

I got in my car and was driving home, having to stop at a gas station since I was almost on empty. Ten minutes down the road, my cell phone rang. I couldn't answer it because I was driving. It rang again. I knew something was going on. I pulled into a filling station and immediately called my sister, Danette, back.

"Daddy's gone," she said. That was it. She didn't say any more.

I burst into tears. Here's the thing with me. I try to live my life with no regrets. What I mean by that is if there's anything I would later wish I had said or done, then I do it right then. If I don't want to do it, or I did what I wanted, then I have no regrets. With my father, I had no regrets. What I wanted to do and say when it came to him, I'd done and said. The only thing I regretted in that exact moment was that I hadn't stayed at the house ten more minutes. I wish I had been there when he had taken his last breath. *Why had I not just stayed ten more minutes?*

I pulled myself together. My husband offered to drive, but I drove back. My daddy was gone. *Daddy was gone.* I was feeling a certain way at this point because I had left him before he left me. I can't explain why I wanted to be there, but I hated I had left when I did.

Then quietly I heard in my spirit, "If you had stayed ten

more minutes, I would have waited, so you still would have been gone. Don't be upset that you weren't here. I love you, Vanessa. I can stand again with no problem." I could just imagine Daddy laughing, standing up, picking up a rod and reel, and casting his line out into the lake for the first time in a long time.

I was okay once I realized that, no matter how long I would have stayed, he was going to wait until I'd left to leave. We (my mother and all five of his children) were all there when they came and took his body away. It was close to midnight now. My mother had been so strong. She handled all that was required with the nurse who processed the legally mandated disposal of all his remaining medicines. When Mama finished, she broke down and let out a guttural cry. Her husband (for seven months shy of sixty years) was gone.

I went to work the next day at 5 a.m. I was working in the vault at Home Depot as a back-office associate (aka bookkeeper) during that time. My store manager came in for my end-of-the-day process verifying of the vault. He was talking and telling me something he wanted me to do after my lunch break. I said, "Let me just tell you this. My father died last night."

"What? Vanessa, I am *so* sorry. Why are you here? Why didn't you call me and call out?" he said. "You shouldn't have come today. Why didn't you call out?"

"Because I know how important this part is to the store, and it would have put you all in a bind to try and get someone in who can do this on such short notice," I said. "My father would have wanted me to come in and do my job. I'll leave when I finish and go do what I can now that this is done." I then broke down and cried. My store manager hugged me as I cried.

At my father's funeral, my middle son, Jeremy (an officer in the army), did a fabulous job in his words of expression. Wearing his regular Army Green Service uniform jacket, he took it off as he spoke and put on his ceremonial Army Blue Service jacket. He said that's what Daddy had done: Changed out of his regular uniform into the upscale one. It was powerful. I spoke, quoting a line from the movie *Black Panther* where the father, T'Chaka, said to his son, T'Challa, "A man who has not prepared his children for his own death has failed as a father." I turned to my father's casket and said, "Daddy, you indeed prepared us. You did not fail as a father."

Now, if this was the end of my story, it would be enough. However, it's not.

As I drove one morning to my 5 a.m. shift, all of a sudden, I just broke down in tears. I then heard my father's voice (in my mind) as I boo-hooed down the freeway. My daddy was saying something about a dime. I had no clue what that was about, but my father was notorious about saving coins. Again, he said something about a dime. I arrived at work not thinking anything more about it.

My first task required me to verify that the count from the previous day matches or is accounted for at the start of a new day. I verified the vault count and the loose funds in the change drawer tray (bills and coins) and continued with my other tasks. At the end of the process, I was pouring the newly counted loose coins into their appropriate change drawer slots when I saw an old Mercury head, winged

Lady Liberty dime on top of the dime heap in the tray. I was certain it wasn't there earlier. I immediately recalled my daddy saying (in my mind) something about a dime. I laughed, went out of the vault to my purse, and got a dime to swap out for that dime.

This still didn't mean anything to me. Not until I started going places and finding dimes on the ground everywhere. I'd be out, look down, and there would be a dime. I was accustomed to finding pennies (you know the saying, "Find a penny pick it up, all day long you'll have good luck."). But I wasn't used to finding silver coins, and especially not dimes.

In November, a co-worker and I went to buy gifts for our store's Christmas party. I parked at Target, opened my car door, stepped out of my car, and there on the ground was over three dollars in silver coins—ninety percent of them dimes. I started laughing as I began picking them up. My co-worker thought I was crazy to be excited about finding coins on the ground. She said I would enjoy myself in the crevices of her couch. I explained the significance and how this was a message from my father. She then understood.

I began to constantly find dimes. In the washing machine, in the dryer, this place, that place. My mother and other family members started having dimes show up for them. My sister Danette, told how—on her birthday—she'd stepped out of the shower and a dime seemingly just fell from the ceiling. My sister Arlinda found her share of dimes. Recently, she won an award for "CBS Remarkable Woman 2023," was packing to fly to Los Angeles, California, and found three dimes in the pocket of her suitcase. My mother has found dimes, even down to when she and I were in France in August of 2021. She'd gone into the bathroom, when she came out, and opened her hand to show me a Euro dime she'd found. It was even happening internationally!

So many dimes were showing up that I began saving them in a container. I presently have over 100 dimes, and that's not counting my earlier finds before I started keeping them.

Some folks may think this is all made up or that it means nothing. If I had been finding dimes all along, I would brush it off too. Whether you believe it's because we're thinking about dimes now that we're manifesting them, then that's fine. It merely proves you can think about something and cause it to manifest. *Me?* I have come to believe that my father made a deal with God to let us know he's still with us in spirit, thinking about us, encouraging us by dropping a dime on us. Yes, we have all witnessed just how much life can turn on a dime.

There was a time back when there were phone booths, we'd put a dime in the slot to make a phone call (of course the price did go up over time). Maybe when Daddy wants to encourage us, there's a way to make dimes show up, putting a dime in something like a phone booth slot, and it drops down to us. Whatever the case, there's something to be said for the love of loved ones. Those who have gone on from this earthly place, figuring out a way to let us know that—when we leave here—this is not the end. It would make sense that the love he had for us wouldn't end just because he stepped from this realm into another.

Maybe someone reading this has had their own signs they either weren't sure of or have wondered about. My

Daddy used to have redbirds (cardinals) show up for him when he was alive that he believed was a proxy loved-one thought or sign. I've seen a few redbirds, but nothing speaks to my heart like these dimes.

While writing parts of this, I confess I've shed some tears. But I'm also ending this with a huge smile on my face. When you can live a life that touches and blesses others, then your living is not in vain. Life can truly turn on a dime: both good and bad. My father on earth (like my Father in Heaven) has given us permission and blessing to live this life to the fullest. From me to you: This is my ten cents' worth as I drop *this* dime on you!

My daddy….my father…our provider…our protector…a part of the foundation on which our family was built (where he constructed it on serving and loving God first) demonstrated how our Heavenly Father loves us, provides for us, and protects us. Daddy wasn't able to go fishing for years; but now (as I imagine him in Heaven), I see him casting his fishing line, smiling, and laughing as he reels in "the big one!"

Meet the Authors

PETER LAST was very nearly born in an elevator and has continued to be unconventional ever since. He began writing his first novel, *Guardians of Magessa*, at the age of eleven, and has since released two trilogies. After earning his degree in Civil Engineering and commission in the United States military, he is now serving in the U.S. Air Force, protecting the nation from its enemies, termites, and HVAC outages. In the little spare time he has, Peter writes a blog, draws, and dabbles in film directing.

ANN H. NUNNALLY is a retired minister, author, and conference speaker. She is the creator and CEO of "An Encouraging Word with Ann Nunnally," a nonprofit, tax-exempt organization established to minister to the body of Christ worldwide through conferences, evangelical outreaches, and writing. In her spare time, she continues to speak at conferences across the globe and contribute weekly to her local newspaper.

JENNIFER HORNE served as the twelfth Poet Laureate of Alabama from 2017 to 2021. She's the author of three collections of poems and a collection of short stories, and she has edited four volumes of poetry, essays, and stories. Her latest work is a biography of the writer Sara Mayfield, forthcoming from the University of Alabama Press.

PETE BLACK hails from Monroeville, Alabama, home of literary icons Harper Lee, Truman Capote and Pulitzer Prize winning journalist Cynthia Tucker. He is a civil engineering graduate from the University of Alabama who is retired after a 35-year career in the pulp and paper industry. Black writes 700-word nonfiction short stories about ordinary people who have overcome obstacles to accomplish extraordinary things. His short stories have been published in two compilations, *Never Lose Heart: Ordinary People Who Refused to Quit* in 2022 and *Never Lose Heart: Sports Heroes Who Overcame the Odds* in 2023.

Alabama dirt lurks stubbornly under the fingernails of lifetime farmer **MIKE WAHL**. More time for writing came only after retiring from a 48-year career working as an aerospace engineer.  With writing efforts concentrated primarily on poetry, his poems have appeared in numerous print and on-line venues in recent years. He released one book of poetry in 2020 and two others in 2021.

DONNA STEELE is an author who strives to be courageous and impeccable with her words. She has worn many hats, including librarian, literacy and reading tutor, and President of the League of Women Voters of Hancock County Indiana. As an opinion writer for the *Greenfield Daily Reporter*, she won first place for Best General Commentary by the Hoosier State Press Association Foundation. In the future, she hopes to pursue her desire to write children's stories.

LAURA HUNTER was raised in Alabama hill country and now lives near Tuscaloosa. She has published sixteen award-winning fiction pieces and nine poems, in addition to the numerous articles published through different media outlets. In 2020, Hunter released a collection of fictional short stories entitled *Southern Voices* which focuses on Copeland's Crossing, Alabama. Hunter's first novel *Beloved Mother*, released April 2019, has won numerous national and international awards.

CHRISTAL ANN RICE COOPER is a newspaper writer, feature stories writer, poet, fiction writer, photographer, and painter. She has been writing for newspapers for over 25 years and currently runs her own personal blog and non-profit website which acknowledges ALL voices, ALL individuals, ALL political views, ALL philosophies, ALL religions.

JUDY BENOWITZ is a creative writer in Cartersville, Georgia with an MA in Professional Writing from Kennesaw State University in Georgia, where she was Who's Who among Students in American Universities and Colleges in 2016. She is the 2015 Creative Writing Contest winner in the Georgia Writers Museum, and her stories appear in GRITS (Girls Raised in the South), the Atlanta Jewish Times, and the Georgia Writers Association among others. Her book *"Descendants,"* available on Amazon, is a collection of essays about her family from the plantation to modern day. She is currently writing a fiction collection.

DR. DANIEL MICHAEL has been a pastor since 1991 and has been at his present church for 23 years. He is the husband of Shelaine Michael, is a father of three and grandfather to five, and lives on a hobby farm with his ninety-plus-year-old parents whom he cares for.

DR. BILL KING is a husband, father, grandfather, ordained minister, humorist, storyteller, speaker, songwriter, singer, musician, published author, syndicated columnist, and cancer survivor. He has published nine books—ranging from Christian novels to animated children's books—as well as recorded five CDs. In 2020, his weekly column placed second at the Southern Christian Writer's Conference, and in 2021, it placed first.

TOM MCDONALD is the author of three books. His first two books, *When Memories Come Calling*, and *Dirt Road Memories*, A Collection of Southern Short Stories, were selected as Southern Region winners in the non-fiction category by the USA Region Excellence Book Awards. The organization recognizes and rewards excellence in books that take the reader into the heart of a 'place.' His third book is titled *Promises To Keep*. The youngest of seven children, McDonald grew up in the Sweetwater community of Florence, Alabama. His entire family were white collar workers. His large extended family and growing up in the 1950's and 1960's in the Deep South are reflected heavily in his writing.

CORINDA MARSH is an author and retired college professor with a Ph.D. in English. Writing the gritty south is her heart and soul, and her 15 publications include her father's memoir and stories of her brother's pioneer skin diver days.

JAMES BREWER is a retired U.S. Army officer and former West Point instructor. He currently teaches writing at Polk State College in central Florida, in addition to his pursuits as a public speaker, musician, and martial artist. As an author, Brewer has written five novels and three non-fiction books.

NANCY HOLDER PRESSLEY was born and raised in Washington, D.C., though she has called east Tennessee home since she was eighteen. Throughout her varied career, she became involved in writing to communicate with target audiences of employees, clients, customers, and the public. In retirement, she is enjoying expressing herself in her own voice.

An author and motivational speaker who adores the power of words both written and spoken, **VANESSA DAVIS GRIGGS** left 18 years of service with BellSouth at the end of 1996 and stepped out on faith as she pursues her purpose and passion—writing and speaking. **She** is the author of 18 novels and has won countless awards for her work. She has most recently facilitatied writing workshops for the Birmingham Public Library, done motivational speaking engagements, and been the keynote speaker for various events.

Did you enjoy reading *Fathers*? If so, please leave an honest review wherever you interact: Amazon.com, Goodreads, or any of your social media platforms.

Gritty Southern Christmas

Bluewater Publication debuted a new brand in fall of 2021 with Gritty Southern Christmas. The 2021 edition of Gritty Southern Christmas Anthology features a wide variety of stories from a wide variety of authors with connections to the South. Bluewater Publications and Gritty South are excited to feature the voices of award-winning authors such as Mike Wahl, Laura Hunter, and Vanessa Davis Griggs; the previous and current Poet Laureates of Alabama, Jennifer Horne and Ashley Jones; as well as some of Bluewater's own authors like Gayle Young, M.E. Hubbs, and Peter Last.

These are not your typical, warm-and-fuzzy, small-town Christmas tales. For some, the holidays are simply not the most wonderful time of the year. While many of us enjoy the festivities of the season, those weeks can also serve to remind us of painful memories and the great voids in our hearts as we ache in silent grief amidst the merriment. From those who have lost loved ones to the story of the mother who works all year to keep her children fed yet has no extra money to put gifts under the tree, this is our writing. Maybe these are your people. No one tells it better than those who have lived it.

To order Gritty Southern Christmas Anthology:
ISBN 9781949711882 – eBook
ISBN 9781949711899 – perfect binding or softback

Gritty South

Established in 2021, Gritty South is an imprint of Bluewater Publications seeking to publish collections of gritty, Southern stories that are not afraid to tell it as it is and display the less attractive, less discussed side to life. We expect that these anthologies will feature renowned and overlooked writers from all over the South.

Check GrittySouth.com

For the release dates of the following Anthologies.
Mother - May 2025
At the Dinner Table/Feeding the Family - March 2026

Submissions are at the discretion of the publication.